THE DO-IT-YOURSELFER'S GUIDE TO SELF-SYNDICATION

Using Secrets, Shortcuts,
Strategies & Psychology
to Get Your Column in Print

ISBN 978-1-60910-181-7

Printed in the United States of America.

in conjunction with
Booklocker.com, Inc.
2010

THE DO-IT-YOURSELFER'S GUIDE TO SELF-SYNDICATION

Using Secrets, Shortcuts,
Strategies & Psychology
to Get Your Column in Print

By: Jill Pertler

Dedication

To my steadfast and loyal editors and proofreaders – my husband, Thom, and kids: Maddie, Jack, Anders and Cal. You all probably fight the urge to run and hide on Sunday evenings when I approach with my printed pages. Instead, you read my words. That helps more than you could know.

Thanks too, for letting me put your stories out there for the world to read. You guys are good sports.

And to the big guy upstairs – keep sending those pennies.

Acknowledgments

Much goes into writing a book. Much more than I ever imagined before sitting down to pen this piece. I want to thank the first publisher who put my name into byline format: Wendy Johnson of the *Cloquet Pine Journal.* When I approached Wendy about writing a column, she could have said "No thanks." If she had, chances are this book never would have been written.

Nikki Willgohs, the best business partner (and friend) ever, helps make my words look good. Whenever I ask her for a favor (like help designing the cover of this book), she comes through in flying colors – sometimes quite literally. Every writer should have a graphic designer by her side. I highly recommend it.

Thanks to my mom and dad for being the greatest. Always.

To the publishers, editors and readers who enjoy *Slices of Life* each week: Wow. I am so glad you do.

THE DO-IT-YOURSELFER'S GUIDE TO SELF-SYNDICATION

Table of Contents

1.

Chapter 1

My story
What worked for me may work for you… or not.

Greetings! My name is Jill Pertler and I am a syndicated columnist. Make that a ***self***-syndicated columnist.

Before getting to the nitty gritty, I have a confession. Self-syndication was never part of my Big Plan (because I didn't have one). I didn't know anything about it before diving into the syndicated world a few years ago. I did my best to figure things out and find the best way to accomplish my goals. Sometimes my methods worked; other times, not so much. But, I learned just as much from my mistakes as my successes. My methods are by no means the only way to do things. They are one way: my way. But, maybe they'll work for you, too.

Confession number two: I am still learning, because my journey is far from over.

Confession number three: My qualifications – or lack thereof. My degree is in psychology, not journalism. I've never been a reporter for a newspaper. Before beginning this process I didn't have connections with numerous newspaper publishers, or have ties with lots of editors. I'd never written, much less published, a book and I didn't have celebrity status or a name that was recognized by many. When it comes to finding success as a syndicated columnist, the odds were stacked against me. At first glance, it would appear I didn't have a whole lot in my favor.

While my resume wasn't brimming, looking back, I did have five important factors needed to find success as a syndicated columnist. They are:

- A love of writing and story-telling,
- The desire to be a columnist,
- A willingness to work hard and not give up (stubbornness?),
- Some writing talent,
- Some luck.

I am a true do-it-your-selfer. I will try anything once. I have wallpapered bathrooms, sewed curtains, canned tomatoes and cut my own hair; I think you get the picture. So, when it came to syndicating my newspaper column, it only made sense that I'd be naïve enough to try it on my own. I've learned as I went – sometimes the hard way, but most often with positive results.

My need to expand the column festered until it became bigger than my lack of confidence.

I am self-syndicated, meaning I am going it alone. There is no conglomerate or professional syndication service standing behind me or showing me the way. Becoming self-syndicated was never part of the Big Plan for me. Looking back, it was a slow and painstakingly gradual process that just sort of unfolded over time. Here's how.

Kid writer to column writer

I've always loved to write. I was the kid who started the elementary school newspaper back in fifth grade. I had a journal when they were called diaries. For as long as I can remember, I've had a love affair with words. But, a love of writing does not make one a good writer. It helps, but the act of loving something does not make you qualified to do it for a living.

I had a small amount of writing successes – enough to make me think that maybe my love was accompanied by at least a smidgen of talent. Love and talent, when combined, still aren't enough to ensure writing success. To do that, you need skill. And skill comes from practice.

I started my career in the corporate world. I wasn't a writer. But, my preoccupation with the craft became evident in my work and I was asked to put together a quarterly company newsletter. It was hailed as a success, and when I left corporate a few years later to stay at home with my two young children, my boss asked if I'd continue to write the newsletter on a contract basis. That was in 1995, the year I officially retired to become a writer. I've been freelancing ever since.

In 2000, I teamed up with a graphic designer to form a marketing, design and copywriting business. We've had opportunities to complete many creative projects over the last decade.

I started writing my column, *Slices of Life*, for my hometown newspaper in 2002. It was a creative endeavor, done purely for my own enjoyment – something I'd always wanted to do. I wrote about a column a month. I loved writing it so much that I knew I wanted to do more, but I was lacking one important ingredient: guts. I was afraid that people out there in the big world beyond my own small town wouldn't like what I wrote. So I went on writing a column a month for the paper I knew and the people who knew me. It was the easy route.

My need to expand the column festered until it became bigger than my lack of confidence. I knew I had to step out of my comfort zone and take a risk or two. I had to prove to myself that I could do it. I set my first short-term goal. I decided to see if I could write a column a week for a year. This involved approaching my hometown newspaper and asking if they could publish me every week. They said, "Yes." (Whew!)

A year went by and low and behold, I'd written a column a week. Goal number-one met and conquered! Looking back, spending a whole year just proving I could write a weekly column seems luxurious. It was. But, it was useful in more ways than just proving to myself I could do it. I established a respectable resume at the same time. My year's-worth of columns not only showed me that I could do it; they showed prospective editors as well.

That's not all. What do basketball players, hockey players, dancers, pianists, vocalists and any other artists or athletes do to get better at their craft? They practice. Even though I was writing professionally, completing a column each week was good practice. It made me better at what I was doing. With every column I learned tricks and techniques. I gained skills

Because I was inexperienced, cheap and a bit of a coward, I decided on the self-syndication route.

for pulling everything together. My words got tighter. The quality improved and I became a better writer – one that was more likely to be a successful columnist beyond my small town of supportive neighbors and friends.

Stumbling upon self-syndication

After writing my weekly column for a year, I did a lot of research regarding syndication. The whole task of finding a syndicate to represent me seemed daunting. Besides, I wasn't an established columnist or an established newspaper reporter. Oh, sure, I'd written a column a week for a year, for my one small town newspaper (circulation about 5,000) but I didn't know if a syndicate would even consider me until I was more experienced.

I didn't know the ins and outs of approaching a syndicate on my own, so I explored having someone else do that for me. There are services that will help you through the syndication process for a fee. They promise to help match you with the syndicate that best meets your needs and vice versa. I was hesitant to spend hundreds of dollars on this type of service when there was no guarantee that I'd even find a syndicate to represent me. (For contact information on this, see the last chapter.)

So, because I was inexperienced, cheap and a bit of a coward, I decided on the self-syndication route. Looking back, I realize that it afforded me a number of pluses.

1. It enabled me to start slowly.
2. It didn't involve huge expenses on my part.
3. I could do everything from my computer. No meetings. No travel.
4. It gave me full control – of where my columns were published and how much I charged.
5. I could do it myself.

Initially, I approached about 30 newspapers in my own home state of Minnesota. After a few months of sending them information, I'd gained two newspapers for a grand total of three. While still tentative, my courage was growing. I began a statewide syndication drive and within six months I grew from 3 newspapers to 32. Each week, my words landed on the doorstep of about 100,000 households. At first, I was afraid to open response emails because I thought editors might blast me for sending them unwanted emails. This never happened. Not all response emails were positive. Some politely asked me to take them off my distribution list. Others weren't as polite, responding with a one-word (capitalized) REMOVE. But, there were the 30-plus editors who responded favorably. They enjoyed my work and had room for it in their newspaper. The good feelings I got from the positive responses far out-weighed the negativity from the "no thank-you" emails and I was hooked.

I have learned a lot along the way about what to do and about what not to do. I've learned that small town newspapers (as well as big city ones) appreciate good writing and a well thought out message.

The opportunity and potential for expansion and success are out there. I am only limited by time. My work continues to grow. As of this writing, my column is published in over 70 newspapers. Not bad for a do-it-yourselfer.

As for you, if you are reading this, chances are you are on the threshold of fame and fortune! You have decided to self-syndicate your column on the topic of (fill in blank here) and will soon be read in households across the nation! All that stands between you and your dream is this business of self-syndication, in other words, a whole lot of hard work. Self-syndication certainly is that, but it can also be a satisfying and successful way to take your writing career to the next level (and beyond).

Good luck!

2.

Chapter 2

Syndication basics

Syndication is an impressive term for a pretty simple concept. It means you can take one column, article or feature and sell it to multiple sources. Pretty cool from a writer's perspective: you write one thing and it's published in lots of places.

I don't know of a writer who doesn't get a happy, warm and fuzzy feeling knowing that people are reading her work. Through syndication, many more people have access to your words. For me, that was the real draw. Oh sure, I want my writing to make me rich someday, but having people (lots of people) read my column? That's a whole new definition of wealth!

A syndicated column (versus one article) is a series of articles that have a common theme. Gardening, food, parenting, education, business, saving money, family matters, advice, home improvement, politics and pets are all possible column topics.

With syndication, newspapers and magazines pay much less for an article than they would if they were paying for first or sole rights to that article. Because newspapers have limited and very defined circulation areas, this works well for them. Unless you sell your column to two papers in the same small town, it is unlikely that they – or you – will run into competition issues.

While you don't get big bucks from one publishing source, the potential is there to get many small paychecks from numerous sources. The math is the same. You can sell one article to a national glossy magazine for $500, or you can sell that same article, in syndicated form, to 20 newspapers for $25 each or 50 newspapers for $10 each. Whether the money comes in all at once, or in many small increments, your checkbook won't know the difference.

Traditional syndication

Traditionally, the act of selling the articles was done through a professional syndication service. A business (known as a syndicate) agrees to represent writers and sells the writers' work to various sources, i.e. newspapers. In return for this service, the syndicate takes a percentage of the fees charged to the newspaper; I'm told around 40 to 50 percent. I'm also told that this is a good deal – if you can get a syndicate to represent you. It isn't easy. From what I read, they reject

Self-syndication is not for everyone.

Some days I wish it wasn't for me.

many columns and accept just a small fraction (one to two percent) of submissions. I was a teeny, tiny fish in a great big pond and didn't figure I had a snowball's chance in you-know-where of catching a syndicate's attention. Looking back, I was probably right.

Working with a syndicate requires that they accept you as a client. You'll sign a contract and agree to certain terms and conditions. Self-syndication is different.

I'm a syndicated columnist!

Anyone can declare him or herself a self-syndicated columnist. There are no requirements or forms to fill out. You can literally wake up one day and say, "I'm a syndicated columnist!" and it is so – sort of. Of course, just because you call yourself something, doesn't make it all fall into place. The only thing easy about self-syndication is declaring it as your title. The rest is all about hard work.

When you self-syndicate, you do all the tasks that a syndication service would do for you. That means you search for and find sources to publish your work. You approach them. You give a sales pitch. You are responsible for ongoing communication and relationship building. You need to develop an approach to get paid. And, you have to keep track of it all.

Self-syndication is not for everyone. Some days I wish it wasn't for me. I'd love to have someone come and find me new sources, print invoices or keep my address book up to date. Some writers – many writers – would rather spend their time working on their column or novel versus the business end of syndication. It can be a lot of work, and it can be work that most writers do not enjoy.

In addition, self-syndication requires another trait that doesn't come easily for me: patience. The editors I contact have never heard of me; they see me as a new writer and a new columnist, without any experience, history or credibility. When a professional syndicate approaches newspapers, those newspapers know who and what they are dealing with. When I approach a newspaper, I am an unknown entity. It takes editors time to get to know me and my work. It takes weeks and weeks of meeting deadlines and sending emails before they decide that I write a high-quality column and am responsible and consistent enough to warrant their attention.

The average person needs to see the same message at least three times (usually more like five to eight) before that message has a good chance of being committed to long-term memory. This is true between columns and editors. It's likely that newspaper editors have to see your name and your columns over and over before they'll even take the time to read one. (Sad, but true.)

An established syndicate may receive a response from a newspaper immediately, or within a week or two. If you decide to self-syndicate, be prepared to wait substantially longer than that. In my experience, I've seen newspapers trickle in a couple at a time. My readership has built gradually, which was okay with me, because I was learning along the way.

Despite some of the challenges, there are definite benefits to self-

Anyone can declare him or herself a self-syndicated columnist. You can literally wake up one day and say, "I'm a syndicated columnist!" The only thing easy about self-syndication is declaring it as your title. The rest is all about hard work.

syndication. It puts you in total control: of your product, compensation and disbursement. You don't have to share your profits with anyone (except maybe your kids and spouse).

Like just about anything that's worth anything in life, self-syndication involves hard work, dedication, diligence, talent and maybe a smidgen or two of dumb luck. If I haven't scared you off yet, keep reading. I've got lots of useful information that can make your self-syndication journey a safe and healthy trip (with maybe just a bump or two in the road).

In case you want to check them out, I've listed the "big five" well-established, well-known syndicates in the resource section in the last chapter.

3.

Chapter 3

Column basics

If you are considering self-syndication, I am going to assume that you already have an established column. Maybe you are published in your hometown paper, like I was. Maybe you have a website or blog that you contribute to on a regular basis (key word here is regular). However you do it, you write regularly and consistently – come sun, rain, sleet, snow or kindergartner with an ear infection.

An idea for a possible column, outlines of columns you plan to write or even two written columns is not sufficient. I recommend having a regular writing schedule for at least six months before taking the syndication leap. If you jump, and fail, it is unlikely that others (a.k.a. newspapers) will give you a second chance. If you make your ascent slow and gradual, you'll be more able to learn from your mistakes, brush yourself off and continue on your way without falling completely flat on your face.

You'll find that writing a column and syndicating that column involves proving yourself over and over – to publishers, editors, other journalists, your readers and yourself. This six-month probationary period is as much about proving things to yourself as to anyone else.

Because I know you have an established column, I'm not going to talk too much about topic. Yours was decided long ago, correct? Suffice to say that topics of general interest (for instance the joys of pet ownership) are preferred over topics geared to a very specific audience (for instance female Dachshund breeders living near Poughkeepsie, New York).

Since you have the established topic for your established column, I am also going to assume that you have a topic file. If you don't, get one. A topic file is just a list of possible column ideas. I give each of my possible ideas its own Word file and then organize all those files in one "possible topics" folder. Sometimes all I have is one sentence for a topic, other times I get four or five paragraphs. When I sit down at my computer to write and my fingers don't want to do any talking, I can go to my possible topics folder and see what's there. Often a story that was started a few weeks earlier will fall into place and my day of lacking column ideas ends with a completed piece.

Length? You want to tell your story – beginning, middle and end – without getting too lengthy. I shoot for 500 to 700 words, but occasionally go over. I do this with two groups of people in mind. The first are readers. We are a down and dirty, give it to me quick society. As a columnist, I don't have 20 minutes to tell someone a story. They want to read it in two or three minutes – five max. So, my columns must be brief.

The second group I'm writing for are the folks at the newspaper. For them, words mean space. With a newspaper, remember that less is often more. It's easier for an editor to place a 600-word column than a 900-word one (and a 350-word column is easier still). If you are over 900 words, I am willing to bet that you could cut at least 100 and leave your story intact. In fact, I bet I could cut 200 words. As you become more experienced as a writer, you will find it easier – and you will become better at – telling your story succinctly without a bunch of word fluff. Repeat the mantra: less is more.

Having said that, I try never to fall below 500 words. Less than that and I feel I'm not giving the newspaper their money's worth. This is the rule for my specific column, however. There are some columns out there – very successful columns – that run between 200 and 300 words. It all depends on your subject matter and your style.

Good writing

A good column tells a story. It has a beginning, middle and end. It defines and describes its scene, characters and action. It is well-written. This last part is imperative. You will not find success as a self-syndicated columnist unless your column is well-written.

There are volumes filled with the how-tos of good writing. If you are considering self-syndication, let's hope you've got most of those how-to's down. Having said that, there are a number of points that every good column should cover. I found a writing checklist of sorts that I can't resist including here. I think it is one that can benefit any writer in just about any writing situation.

Mark Twain penned a list of "18 rules governing literary art" when critiquing a novel by Fenimore Cooper, but I think much of it generalizes to column writing. Because Samuel Clemens (Twain) has been dead more than 70 years, this list is no longer protected by copyright (more on that in chapter 13). In fact, you can find it all over the Internet. I have taken liberties with the list, paraphrasing and combining some of the

A good column tells a story. It has a beginning, middle and end. It is well-written. This last part is imperative.

points, to come up with a list of 14 rules here. (You might say I've given the list a fresh coat of paint.) Twain's ideas are in italics, with my own comments following each point. Twain used the word "story," in his rules. As you read, substitute the word "column." As far as this list goes, for our purposes the two words are interchangeable. If you would like to see Twain's original list (in its entirety and in his own words) check it out online at any number of sites, including this one:
http://jprof.com/editing/twainoncooper.html

Twain's list

Twain starts out by referencing the 19 rules governing literary art in the domain of romantic fiction. He then goes on to list 18. Try as I might (and I have tried) I cannot find the elusive number 19. Whether you write romantic fiction or a syndicated column, in 1900 or the new millennium, I think these are rules to write by. Every day.

1. A story should accomplish something and arrive somewhere. There's that beginning, middle and end I was talking about. Your column needs a beginning that makes readers want more, a middle that tells them a story and an ending that comes out of nowhere to make them sit up and feel surprised, happy and/or contemplative – but by all means satisfied.

2. Each paragraph – each sentence – of a story should be necessary. You don't want to waste a reader's time. If a detail really happened, but has no bearing on the outcome of your story, leave it out. This touches on the importance of editing. We'll talk about that next.

3. Characters in a story should be alive, except in the case of corpses. Readers should be able to distinguish corpses from others. This rule would be humorous, if it weren't so darn true. Your column needs no dead characters (unless they really are dead). Why? Alive characters who act dead are boring.

4. Characters – both dead and alive – should have a reason to be in the story. We're back to making every sentence count. The same goes for people. If you mention someone, they better have a key role in your message. If not, leave them out.

5. Dialogue should sound like real conversation. It should fit the character and have a meaning, purpose and relevancy. It should be interesting, on topic, help to tell the story and stop before it gets boring. Dialogue is a tough one for many writers. How to make it real? One of my college writing professors advocated for eavesdropping on conversations. It's kind of fun. If you use dialogue, use it with purpose – only when nothing other than dialogue will do. One way to make sure it sounds and feels natural is to read it out loud.

6. Avoid crass stupidities. This goes without saying. Readers dislike crass stupidities because they are crass and stupid. They may even find them insulting. Never insult your reader.

7. The story told should be possible and reasonable. As a columnist, you may take some liberties with the actual facts because it helps you tell your story better, more succinctly etc. But, make sure that any changes you make are plausible.

8. Say exactly what you want to say. Nothing more. Nothing less. Good advice.

9. Use exactly the right word. So true. Use your thesaurus as a tool, not a crutch.

10. Avoid being too wordy. Be brief. Couldn't have said it better myself. More on editing soon. (I know you can't wait!)

11. Include necessary details. It can be tricky: being brief while including impressive details. Tricks are fun, but only when mastered.

12. Avoid sloppy writing. Thorough, thorough proofreading is the best prescription for sloppy writing. Reading your own words out loud is a great technique to help you clean them up. A dictionary helps, too.

13. Use good grammar. There is no excuse for bad grammar. The smallest mistakes will cast shadows upon your image with editors, publishers and readers.

14. Use a simple, straightforward style. Say what you want to say; don't beat around the bush. Whenever you have the choice, choose simple prose over complex, compound sentences. If you can't say it simply, perhaps it's better left unsaid – or unwritten.

Editing

Editing provides a number of benefits to you and your column. It takes the word countdown (say from 900 to 700) and makes your column size more attractive to papers. It makes your writing tighter. You say what you need to say, using only the words you need to use. It makes your writing error-free; spelling and grammar should be perfect after your editing is complete. It makes you a better writer because it forces you to look at your work – word by painstaking word.

Get in the habit of editing and proofing your column. Be brutal. Remember that with syndication, one error printed in 50 papers totals 50 errors. Ouch! I type my column using Microsoft Word. When finished, I use the Spelling and Grammar feature (under Tools). This highlights possible misspelled words, passive sentences, sentence fragments and more. It also gives you information on word count, readability and reading level.

With passive sentences, I shoot for two percent or less. If a particular column has more than that, I go through it, paragraph by paragraph, using the grammar feature to identify the passive sentences. I don't always change all of them to active tense, but I want to make sure that when I do use a passive sentence I am writing it deliberately, with good reason.

During the editing process, I often do a search for adverbs. I do this by using the Find function under the Edit tab. I type in "ly" and hit "Find next." As with passive sentences, I don't remove all adverbs. I only want to double check that my adverbs aid the column and are used in a planful way.

When it comes to readability, it is imperative that I come in under an eighth grade reading level. Why? It's the reading level of the average American. But that's not all. The purpose of my column is to entertain. If it is filled with complex sentences, convoluted prose and is hard to read or understand, that sort of defeats the purpose of entertaining readers, doesn't it? Someone asked me once if I felt it was annoying to have to "dumb down" my prose to get the readability to an acceptable low level. My answer? Of course not! It is a challenge to make things simple, yet interesting, with an overall message that goes well beyond the column's reading level. Eighth grade? That's nothing. My columns average around a sixth grade reading level. (And I'm proud of it!)

When it comes to grammar and writing style, I follow the rules of the

We are a down and dirty, give it to me quick society. As a columnist, I don't have 20 minutes to tell someone a story.

Associated Press. *The Associated Press Stylebook and Briefing on Media Law* is never far from my computer (my writing space of choice). It's like an old friend who has all the answers to any question that I might ask. The solutions to all life's mysteries: formatting numbers, lie versus lay and any sort of punctuation conundrum I come up with can be found within the boundaries of my *AP Stylebook*. If you don't have one, you want one.

If you can find yourself a proofreading buddy, go for it! Having someone else read your words can help identify errors that you may never see. I often corral family members as proofreaders. So long as they can read at an eighth grade level, they are fair game. At my house that includes just about everyone except the dog and cat.

Having someone proof my work is great, but I'm still my own best editor. One of my most valuable editing tools is my own voice. Cadence is an important factor to my stories. It adds another layer and increases quality – often in a subtle way that's appreciated by readers. I read my column out loud at least four or five times before ever publishing. It helps me find words that are repeated too often, sentences that flow better if restructured and anything else that just doesn't sound quite right. Each time I read the words out loud, I make changes – slight ones, but each change makes the column better. And, one word change for the better is a word change worth making.

Naming your baby

Your column needs a title that is snappy and communicates your topic. The first rule? Say it in as few words as possible. No one wants to read a ten-word title. Go for three words or less, unless you need to use four or five. (Don't you love how the rules always bend here?)

Play around with your topic, your name and fun words that describe your column. What do you want to put in your byline? If you have an especially common name – John Johnson or Sue Smith – you might want to consider editing to make it less common. You could use your middle name or middle initial. John Forrest Johnson could become John Forrest, or John F. Johnson. Some writers just the first initial of their first name: Sue Smith could go by S. Veronica Smith, for instance. If your last name could be hard to pronounce – Mapother or Twyndynling for instance, you could use your first and middle names. While not a writer, Tom Cruise Mapother did this with fairly good success.

Your birth certificate may designate you as Robert Steven Brown, but will you be Rob, Robby, Bob or Robert? Consider the topic of your column. Is it serious, Robert-type stuff or do your words have a lighter, Bobby flair?

Why play with your name? You want to have something that is distinctive, without being too difficult. Name recognition is the ticket, baby, and what you say and how it sounds really does make a difference one way or another.

When you've narrowed your column and name choices down to a few, run your ideas by others, saying them out loud. The last thing you want to do is come up with a tongue twister or something that is difficult to say. Choose your title carefully. Your column may change each week, but your title will stick with you through it all – and hopefully that's a very long time.

Formatting

Because you'll be emailing your column, you don't have complete control over what it will look like on the receiving end. Sometimes, cyberspace messes up your spacing, fonts etc. So, I advocate for simple formatting. I use block-style paragraphs that are justified left. They are typed single spaced, with an extra space between paragraphs.

I use a basic, universal san-serif font like Arial or Helvetica at a size of 11 points. I don't typically use a lot of bolded or italicized words, but when I do, I explain this in the body of my email note. For instance, I might say: "In the third paragraph, I have bolded the word tiger."

Above the column, in the same 11-point Arial, I type the date, double space, the title *(Slices of Life),* double space, the column's name for that week, double space and then the byline.

FOR INSTANCE

People get creative with words when naming their column. It's like adding another layer to the depth and meaning of your subject matter.

Alliteration:
Betty's Baking Basics, Veteran's Voice and
Nurse's Notes.

Rhyme works:
LeRue's Views, Food for the Brood and *Jen's Top Ten*

Cadence can be a positive factor:
Living Well Eating Well,
Check It Out (a column about the local library)
Location, location, location (realtor's column)

Name recognition is like the credit card commercial; it's priceless. Some columns that include names:
Dear Abby, Rod's Ramblings, Ellen Goodman
and *Dave Barry*

Cute and humorous plays on words are fun:
Family Daze, The Principal's Principles, Sew Simple,
Eating In and (of course) *Slices of Life*

At the end of the column, I double space and include my bio information. I keep it short – no more than 50 words. You want to include your name, credentials, website information and an invitation to email or provide feedback. Because I am also promoting my marketing business, I include a short blurb on that as well.

Regarding those credentials: you don't have to have a master's degree in journalism to succeed as a syndicated columnist. I don't. I have a degree in psychology with a minor in creative writing. While I believe my educational background prepared me for column writing, my degree isn't at the top of my credential list. I don't even mention it in my bio. I've spent more years writing than I did in school, so that experience tops my list. If you are fresh out of school with a Master of Fine Arts in Writing, your education very well may be at the forefront of your bio. Sometimes, it's good to tie your bio information in with the subject matter of your column. If you write about gardening, perhaps it is pertinent that you grew up on a farm. If you write about serious business matters, you probably want to keep the bio professional and to the point. My columns often attempt to be humorous, so I could include some funny or quirky fact about my wacky family. You want to use those few sentences to tell something interesting about you and give a flavor of your column in order to sell your product.

Write out a couple of ideas, sample bios, and run them by your family and friends. Which do they prefer? It's always best to get a second (and third and fourth) opinion when you can.

I'd recommend keeping a file of your bios as they change and evolve over time. (They will, believe me!) While you want to keep the information at the end of the column brief, there may be occasions when you need a longer bio. For instance, some newspapers want to include a longer paragraph of information the first time they run a column. It's good to have a variety.

After the bio information, I double space and then type "End," with the word count in parenthesis: End (711).

FOR INSTANCE

Here are examples of bios I've used:

1. Jill Pertler – award-winning freelance writer, syndicated columnist, wife, mother of four and feeder of pets, not necessarily in that order – has written hundreds of articles for various local, regional and national publications. She appreciates your comments and can be reached at pertmn@qwest.net, or you can check out her website at http://marketing-by-design.home.mchsi.com/.

2. Jill Pertler is a syndicated columnist and award winning freelance writer working with graphic designer Nikki Willgohs to provide writing, design and other marketing services to businesses and individuals. You can check out their website at http://marketing-by-design.home.mchsi.com/, e-mail Jill at pertmn@qwest.net or visit *Slices of Life* on Facebook.

And for newspapers asking for a little more information:

3. Jill Pertler's Slices of Life columns are written for regular folks, like her, who know the meaning of hard work, do their best with what they have, love their families with their whole heart and somehow manage to squeeze in time to appreciate and laugh at the small moments that make life worthwhile. One should never be too full for dessert. You don't have to eat the whole pie, but you probably have room for a small slice.

Jill appreciates your thoughts and comments (especially of the positive variety). Email her at pertmn@qwest.net.

4.

Chapter 4

Why (self) syndication?
Long-term goals

Before ever syndicating your column, you need to know why you want (dare?) go down this treacherous road. What do you hope to accomplish? Are your goals monetary? Are you working to establish a fan/reader-base? Is a column part of a bigger platform you are building? Will you use the column to establish yourself as an expert in a certain area? Build on a secondary business? Are you looking for fame and fortune? Have you always liked the name Erma? Your goals for the column will impact the way you approach and work with publication sources, so do some soul-searching, and get a straight view on where you are coming from and why.

It seems like an obvious goal choice: a syndicated column should earn you money. We all need to buy groceries. The significant feature of a syndicated column over a traditional article is that you have the potential to be paid over and over for one 600-word essay. Ka-ching! I like the sound of them bananas! Being paid is a great thing. I opt for it whenever I can and money was definitely part of my goals when I decided to syndicate my column.

I have found, however, that not every newspaper has money in its budget to pay columnists. This is a sad, real-world truth. A happy, real-world truth is that the rewards of a syndicated column don't have to come solely in the form of a paycheck. There are many benefits to writing a column and lots of them can lead to a money trail. It just may not be a direct trail; that is, you may gain business and income because you write your column, but not directly from newspapers paying you to write that column. Sounds complicated, but it isn't, really.

A column can help you establish a fan or reader-base. If people read your words week after week, they come to know you – and hopefully like you. When you publish your book, guess who is going to be first in line to buy it? You've got it, your faithful readers. If you already have a book out there, your column can draw readers to it.

A column can establish you as an expert on a certain topic or help you build your platform. You write about home remodeling projects. People read your advice and use it themselves. Pretty soon, your expertise is recognized and you are asked to speak (for a fee) at the home and garden show. Someone sees you at the garden show and you are asked to be a guest on a local morning cable talk show and this leads to a radio interview. Your success there leads to more radio and TV appearances throughout your state – and beyond. And to think that it all started with your column.

A column can serve as free advertising space to help build a secondary business. In addition to my syndicated column, I have a copywriting and marketing business that I run with a partner who is a graphic designer. I note this information in my bio at the end of each column, with an invitation to readers to check out my website, which showcases many of the marketing projects my business partner and I have completed over the years. Readers see this, and hopefully think of me when they have the need to create a brochure, annual report or newsletter. If I were to take out an ad in each of the papers that runs my column each week, we'd be talking thousands of dollars. I get all this exposure at no cost.

Some people write a column because they are looking for fame and fortune. This was not one of my goals, but it is something that can come out of the whole process of gaining a fan-base. (And it is sort of fun when strangers see you at the supermarket and point and whisper and you know it's not because your zipper is down or that you have a piece of spinach stuck between your teeth.)

Be prepared. Because you will have a photo that accompanies your column (more on that later) people – strangers – will recognize and approach you. Some may even feel like they know you. When this happens, it can be intimidating and overwhelming. Many writers (me included) are much more comfortable hiding behind their words, not speaking in public (to strangers, nonetheless). But, once you get used to it, having people approach you because they enjoy your work can also feel flattering, humbling and downright amazing.

While a syndicated column has a potential for fortune and fame, I believe a fair amount of passion has to be at its base. Some of your rewards have to be intrinsic. For me, it is like knowing that my heart is beating or that I have to breathe. My passion for writing is just there. I don't have to summon it from deep within. It just is.

I've always wanted to write a column. I've always wanted to have people read my words. That passion is my starting point.

Do I want money in my bank account? Sure I do. But, my main reason for writing is to see my words in print. It's hard to describe without sounding like a starving artist. I get off on having people read my words. I really get off when they like what they read. Paychecks? Yeah, they've started to come in, but readers are the real reason why I write.

In all honesty, a syndicated column is tough business. I wouldn't advise getting into it simply for the cash. There has to be more.

The cash may come eventually – and I think it is more likely to come for those who write out of passion. If you love what you are doing, keep doing it. Money is likely to follow passion, but it doesn't often work the other way around.

Your reasons for wanting to syndicate a column will be personal, and can only be decided by you. But, this is something you should think about – honestly. Why, really, do you want your face, words and name out there? For most of us, there is more than one answer to this question. For me, it's a little bit about money, a little bit about self-promotion and a lot about the passion of having others read my words. Thinking about your own personal whys can impact your overall approach as well as the way you look at your outcomes and successes.

Have a pen and paper handy when you do your soul-searching and jot down your thoughts. Assess your goals as well as your passion. Both are important. They should work to balance each other (in the best of circumstances). Passion for writing is good; and it's even better when accompanied by real-world goals. Your can set your goals based on income that your column brings in, but just as important (and rewarding)

It is sort of fun when strangers see you at the supermarket and point and whisper and you know it's not because your zipper is down or that you have a piece of spinach stuck between your teeth.

might be setting goals involving number of newspapers that publish the column, overall circulation of the column, speaking engagements you receive as a result of the column and/or an increase in jobs and income from a secondary business that you "advertise" each time your column is printed.

Make your goals short-term (one month, three months, six months) and long term (one year, five years). If you only focus on the five-year goal, you may feel discouraged, and it may start to feel unattainable. It's important to see the small picture as well as the big one.

Measuring your progress

When I first started syndicating my column, it was distributed only in my home state of Minnesota. I got a large map of the state, framed it and hung it right next to my computer. Each time a new paper emailed to let me know they wanted to use my column, I placed a small round sticker on the map where the newspaper was located. On the days when I felt discouraged, and perhaps questioned the whole self-syndication labyrinth, I only needed to look up at the map and the growing group of little round stickies to remind myself that not only was I headed for success – I was already there.

Goals are good, and they can help you see progress over time. Self-syndication can be a gradual process that's completed in baby steps. Keeping track of your goals helps you see those tiny steps and gives you knowledge that you really are moving forward, and that's exactly the direction you want to be going.

5.

Chapter 5

Compensation considerations

It's great to write and be published. It's even better to have others read (and enjoy!) your work. Ah, but we all know the cupcake isn't complete without the icing. In this case, icing often equals money. It's the pinnacle to write, be published, be read and to cash a paycheck at the end of the week.

What is the best way to translate your words into money? To be honest, I'm not sure. Many newspapers are struggling to survive. The world of print journalism is changing and evolving as we speak. There isn't always icing (a.k.a. money) to pay columnists. What to do, what to do?

First, I recommend having a plan of action for the newspapers that are interested in your work, but do not have money to pay you. As I see it, you have two options: you tell them no, or you tell them yes. There is no right or wrong answer here – just the answer that works best for you. Do you say “no” to a newspaper that can get you into 5,000 households every week because they can't pay you? Do you become known as the columnist who will write for free? It's sticky stuff, to be sure.

And, it's sticky stuff that you should chew on, like a good piece of bubble gum, until you come up with the answer that works best for you. If you decide only to work with papers that can pay you, do so with confidence; if you opt for the other route, proceed forward knowing that you are doing what is best for your writing future. In other words, go for it and don't look back! There will be plenty of people telling you that they'd do things differently. And so they can – when they syndicate their own column. You do what's right for you.

When you do get paid, how much should it be? With syndication, the amount paid for articles is less than if you were selling that same article to just one source. It's a win-win situation. Newspapers pay less for a quality article. You get paid over and over. Because the circulation areas of newspapers don't typically overlap, you don't run into territorial issues. You want to keep this in mind, however. You probably don't want to offer your column to two papers in the same small town. Neither one will be happy with you.

I love cashing big paychecks. But, I've found that with syndication, most of the checks are not in the triple digits. That's okay, because of the magic of syndication. If one paper pays me $500 for an article, I have $500. If I can get 50 papers to pay me $10 each, I still have $500. The magic of syndication is that I don't have to stop there. I can sell that same article to 100 papers or 500 or 1,000.

I do think that newspapers – even those with money in the budget to pay columnists – are thrown off by larger compensation requests. I try to keep my fees low enough so that just about anyone should be able to come through with a paycheck. I offer weekly and monthly rates with the monthly rate being equal to the price of two or three columns. For now, I've settled on $10 per column or $25 for the month (bargain discount). Just about everyone can afford $10, can't they? And, like I said in the paragraph above, if I can get 50 newspapers to pay $10 each, I have $500. For a 600-word article, that ain't bad.

From what I read online, my figures may be low. But, I've been doing this for three years now and they don't seem low in the real world. However, there are bloggers and syndication "experts" out there that claim you shouldn't settle for less than $40 a column. I have not found that to be accurate, but this is not science; it's syndication.

I do believe that newspaper editors want to pay columnists if they can. Editors are writers, too – often underpaid writers. They want to compensate the craft, if possible. Even though it's hard to talk about the "M" word, I think it's best to be upfront and honest with editors. I've learned just to ask: "Do you have money in your budget to pay columnists? If so, how much can you pay me?" It works. I get straightforward answers, and not once has an editor gotten mad or upset when I bring up the subject of money. They are refreshingly honest and 99-percent of the time are willing to pay me as much as they can for my work.

Some columnists base their fees on circulation. For instance, newspapers with a circulation of 5,000 or less pay $5 per column, 5,000 to 20,000 pay $10 and those over 20,000 pay $20. I opted not to do things this way for a couple of reasons. First, it's more complicated than a flat fee. I don't like complicated math. I am a writer, not a mathematician. Second, I've found that some of the bigger papers run on the tightest budgets. Charging the larger papers more may only serve to limit my distribution to them (and has the potential to greatly decrease my circulation numbers).

There are other creative things you can do with compensation. Because I am promoting my business with my column, I have bartered for free advertising in lieu of payment. Another option is to provide incentives to newspapers that are the first to give your column a trial run. Perhaps you offer a free six-month trial to the first 10 papers to respond to your query. A trial period gives you the chance to prove how useful and valuable your column can be. When the trial is finished, it is likely that the paper will be motivated to find a way to continue publishing your column. You could offer newspapers a 50-percent reduced rate for the first three or six months. As I said above, I offer a monthly (discounted) rate in addition to a weekly rate. Many newspapers take me up on it, and quite honestly, it simplifies billing on my end.

If an editor really likes your work, he or she may want to get a local business to sponsor your page. For instance, if you write a parenting column, maybe the children's clothing store will pay $100 per month to sponsor your column. For this fee, the newspaper prints your column, along with a small ad on the page noting that business' sponsorship. You get $50 and the newspaper gets $50. Everyone's happy. The kicker to this one is that the editor has to go above and beyond in finding a sponsor for your column. It isn't realistic to think that you as the columnist can do this task. Finding local sponsors is going to require someone who is local. It's the one part of do-it-yourself that you really can't do.

Any gimmick – if it gets an editor's attention and gets your column published and you paid – is a gimmick worth repeating.

I currently send my column to over 1,000 newspapers. I have found

Even though it's hard to talk about the "M" word, I think it's best to be upfront and honest with editors. I've learned just to ask: Do you have money in your budget to pay columnists?

that not every newspaper that wants to use my column has money in its budget to pay me. Do I let them publish without payment because increased readership will help my book be a best seller someday? Or, do I hold out for the cash because my daughter is starting college next year and the tuition isn't going to pay for itself? It's a consideration, and a personal one. But, it's one you should plan for ahead of time.

Whatever you decide, I think it's good to have a goal: 10 papers at $50 per column or 50 papers at $10 per column. However you add it up, at my house it adds up to a chunk of college tuition. Maybe you desire a certain hourly rate. If your column (including writing, editing and administration time) takes you five hours to complete each week and you want to be paid $50 per hour, you'll need to bring in $250 per week. Whether that comes from five papers or 25, the choice is yours.

6.

Chapter 6

Getting a headshot

You might be thinking, "An entire chapter on getting one photograph of... me?" My answer is, "Yep. A whole chapter because the photo is that important."

You want people to read your column. In order for them to take time out of their day to read words on paper, something is going to have to attract their attention. That something is your face – a photo of it, at least. People are drawn to faces. You want yours to be human, inviting and a reflection of your column.

Okay, so now you are thinking that if the photograph of your smiling face is so important, why not go to a professional photographer and get it done right? Good question. You may want to schedule a professional session with a photographer. It's your call. In some cases, though, I think a professional shot does nothing more than make you look like a realtor. I mean no ill will against all the hard-working great-looking realtors out there, but as a writer, you don't need to look perfect. Aim to look like the new neighbor down the street who everyone is anxious to meet.

The photo in question is going to be small (about one-inch square), probably in black and white with the grainy texture that we all associate with newspapers. This is not a perfect system. Depending on the subject matter of your column, a suit and tie are probably not required. You are an artist! Unless the topic of your column is about being a realtor (or maybe a banker) you might want to consider taking your own photo, in an environment where you are comfortable. The most important thing about your photo (in my opinion) is that people see it, recognize that it is you and think, "I'd like to know what she has to say!"

Seeing yourself for who you really are

Making a photo look like you is easier said than done, and it gets harder as the years go by. Believe me. I had a number of photo sessions, with various members of my family serving as photographers, and they all had one problem: none of the photos looked like me. My hair looked too dark (or light). It was too curly, or too straight. My eyes were too small (alas, never too big). I looked tired or bored or too happy or maybe I wasn't wearing enough make-up (or maybe too much)? I had to face facts: I looked way older in the photos than I did in real life (as least I thought so). How to fix that?

I looked at myself in the mirror – really looked – and recognized a couple of problems. My hair needed a trim. I made an appointment. Make-up or no make-up, my eyes really were small. I'd always taken photos of myself without my glasses, but I put them on, looked in the mirror and honestly had to admit that they minimized the fact that my eyes are puny. My point here? Don't be afraid to think outside the lens and make a few changes – even ones like wearing your glasses.

When you are looking in that mirror, experiment with smiles. Teeth or no teeth? Very, very happy or simply content? How do you want to appear? How do you want your readers to see you?

Turn your head slightly from side to side. Consider how you have your hair parted. Is it in the middle or on the side? This might provide for a better vantage point – right or left. Look for skin wrinkles or folds – especially in your neck as you turn your head. You never think you have them, until they stare back at you from a photo – or mirror.

Atmosphere, ambience and lighting

While you're embracing (or re-inventing) your look, consider clothing. A suit and tie says one thing, a Nike T-shirt another. As a columnist, you are a communicator. What do you want to say? A turtleneck says northern exposure and can cover up minor flaws in your chin and neck area. A low sweeping neckline (complete with cleavage) sends another message and may serve to highlight the flaws that your turtleneck covers. Think before you dress – for your headshot, that is.

Do certain colors look better on you than others? If you are unsure, chances are your closet can give you a hint. Is it full of blues? Pinks? It is likely that you most often wear a color that looks good on you. If you're still unsure, stand in front of your friend, the mirror, and hold a few different colored clothing items up to your face. Do not pick the one that makes you look washed out and sallow. Go for the one that seems to add color to your cheeks. Even though the photo used in the newspaper will most likely be black and white, you want to pay attention to color. You will want to use this same photo to establish face, name and column recognition by placing it in other locations – such as your website and social networking sites.

Don't worry about pants or skirts. They aren't going to show up in your headshot anyway. Focus on the shirt, sweater, etc. Go with a solid color; stay away from flashy florals, loud patterns or high contrast stripes. They will take the attention away from Y-O-U, and you are what this headshot is all about.

Wait for a nice day. The lighting is always better and easier to work with outdoors. This is true, unless it is a cloudy winter day in northern

Minnesota or a very rainy day in Seattle. It was cold and cloudy when I took my photo. So, I moved from the outdoors into my dining room. I am telling you this to illustrate (again) that is there are no real wrong or rights with self-syndication. As soon as I say you should always do something (like take your photo outside) we will be confronted with a two-week string of rainy days that force you and your camera inside.

But, in ideal conditions, look for a day when the sun is shining with maybe a few clouds overhead. Find a nice green space outside – in front of trees, bushes or even tall grass. Nature has a way of providing a perfect backdrop.

If you are forced indoors, look for a simple background – a wall that's painted white or cream, for instance. A wooden door may provide a more natural looking background. You want to stand out from, not blend into the background, so look for a background color that is different from your clothing. Stay away from wallpaper or a wall that has photos or other items displayed on it. Look carefully for distractions that could take attention away from you – wall outlets, electric cords, etc.

If possible, choose a room with natural light (a window). You don't have to stand in front of the window to benefit from the natural light it provides. You can experiment with opening the curtains or blinds and leaving them partially closed. Try shutting off the electric lights in the room and shooting with the just natural light. The results might surprise you.

As a writer, you don't need to look perfect. Aim to look like the new neighbor down the street who everyone is anxious to meet.

Taking the photo

If you are the ultimate do-it-yourselfer, like me, you will set your camera on a table and use the self-timing mechanism to take your own shot. That's what I did. As an easy alternative, have your husband, son, daughter or best friend snap about 100 of you. One is bound to look nice.

Whether the camera is set on a table, or held by your son, make sure it is level with your face. Taking the shot from above or below can distort the image and make you look less-than-perfect. The distortion can even make it look like you've added on pounds. (!!)

You want your smile to look natural – not contrived. When I took my shots, I tried thinking happy thoughts and even repeated happy phrases as I was clicking the shutter button. I said things like: "I sure love writing!" "My column is the best!" and "It's so fun to take pictures!" I think you get the picture (sorry, couldn't resist). I felt kind of silly, talking to myself while taking my own photo, but it served to lighten the atmosphere (which is interesting, since I was the only one in the room). Because my column is often humorous, silly was good for my photo. And all that chatter helped me to look more natural – more like me (the young me).

Just about everyone has a digital camera, and I'm assuming that's what you'll use to take your photo. Most digitals offer a choice of picture modes. For instance, there is one mode for photos that involve moving subjects (often called sports mode), another for close up shots and one for shots that include multiple subjects. You can also turn the flash on, turn it off or let your camera decide for you. For more information on the features of your specific camera, I recommend reading your manual.

My point in mentioning the whole spectrum of camera features is to encourage you to try a few. Use the sports mode, portrait mode and the automatic camera mode. Take a few photos with the flash. Then take some with the flash turned off. You might be surprised at the outcome. I find that with close-up shots (like the headshot you are taking) the flash tends to wash out most faces. At least it does mine. By testing out the different modes, you are experimenting with shutter speed and lighting, and the only way to know which looks best (crisp, in focus and well-lit) is to get to know your camera by giving them all a go and then viewing the results on your computer screen.

Did you know that the left side of the face is slightly different from the right side? For this reason, it's hard for most of us to look good in a full, front-on headshot. Take a profile or a slightly off-center shot. Experiment. Turn this way. Then that. Smile with teeth, and without. Give yourself a variety of choices. Tilt your head up and then down. This is especially important for people who wear glasses. You want to avoid glare from the light source. If you have someone taking your photo, you can have him or her check to make sure your glasses are free from glare. If you are alone, like I was, your best bet is to keep tilting and keep pressing the shutter key. Over and over and over.

The great thing about digital cameras is they make taking your own photos easier than ever before. You can see your images immediately and there's no waiting for film to be developed. You can take literally hundreds of shots – and I recommend doing so. The more you take, the more you have and the more likely that at least one will look good enough to print.

Many digital cameras give you a choice regarding photo quality. What this means is that higher quality photos take up more storage space – on your memory card, on your computer and when you send via email. Having said that, I recommend taking photos at the highest quality. You can always decrease the quality later, but you can't reverse it and go the other way around.

Different formats for different uses

Once you have your one great and perfect photo, you'll want to format it in different ways so you can conveniently use it for different applications to promote your column. When you are done, you'll have a folder filled with a number of options:

- One large file for printing large color photos that can be used for numerous promotional materials including things like posters.
- The same large file, but in black and white, for instances when color photos aren't an option.
- One file formatted for newspaper use.
- One small (2 by 2 inch) photo formatted for web use.
- A larger (5 by 5 inch) photo for web use.

Full-size, full-color

It might be hard to imagine your face on a poster or other large, promotional print materials, but this can (and will) happen! Having one large, full-color shot allows you to edit it in any way. You can make it smaller if needed. More importantly, you can print it large for those big projects in your future.

This photo will basically be the shot that you took with your camera. You don't want to decrease the size in any way. Keep it as large as possible. Cropping is optional and based on the specific shot. It's your call.

You'll want to take this same shot and convert it to a black and white image, for those projects that won't allow color. Again, this black and white image can always be altered and made smaller, depending on your needs. For now, keep it as large as possible.

Formatting your headshot for newspapers

Making it email and internet-friendly

Formatting your photo so that it easily traverses through email and is a cinch for newspaper editors to access is going to mean extra work on your part. Why bother with this step? It makes life easier for newspaper editors and graphic designers. Many digital cameras have many mega pixels and are able to take very high quality photos. This is great if you are blowing up your images to poster size. Newspapers don't need poster size, and all that the mega images do for them is gum up their email by taking up lots of storage space.

In addition, by sending a cropped, correctly-sized photo, you are ensuring that your headshot looks consistent from newspaper to newspaper. If you send an uncropped shot of you from the waist up, some papers may use the shot exactly as you send it. Others will crop. Your photo will look different from newspaper to newspaper and that does not help to build a consistent image, which leads to name and column recognition.

dpi, ppi and bytes

First, a quick overview of the technical stuff regarding digital cameras, images, newspapers, cyberspace and how they all view photo resolution.

Resolution refers to the image quality of a photo. High resolution equals high quality. Trouble is, each different source – camera, newspaper and computer – has its own lingo for describing resolution.

Digital cameras measure photo size in pixels – or tiny, light-sensitive squares. The number of pixels lined up right next to each other that it takes to equal one-inch is referred to as points per inch (or ppi). Usually,

Resolution refers to the image quality of a photo. High resolution equals high quality. Trouble is, each different source – camera, newspaper and computer – has its own lingo for describing resolution.

point-and-shoot cameras don't complicate matters too much by talking about ppi. Instead, they refer to photo quality – Good, Better and Best. The photos taken at the Best quality mode have a higher ppi than the ones that are taken in the Good mode.

When it comes to printing images onto paper, the common terminology is dpi, or dots per inch. This refers to the number of dots of ink (per inch) when the image is printed using an ink jet printer. Typically, newspapers like to have photos set at 300 dpi for high-resolution, photo-quality printing.

Computers have a language all their own. They measure the size of photos (and other files) using bytes. You most often hear the terms kilobyte (equal to eight bytes) and megabyte (equal to 1024 kilobytes). You don't have to remember those numbers. Just know that a megabyte is lots bigger than a kilobyte. Bytes don't refer to resolution, just the overall size of a computer file (or photo). But, when you are sending images through cyberspace, size does matter. You will want to pay attention to how the resolution of your photos impacts the number of bytes that they take up on your computer. (Higher resolution equals more bytes.)

So what does all this mean? Newspapers want photos sent at high quality (resolution), so you want to set your camera to take high-resolution photos. These photos will be larger and take up more space – on your camera, on your computer and when sent via email. It isn't courteous to send huge images or files via email, so it will be your job to take your high quality (large) photo and reformat it so that it retains enough quality (resolution) while being small enough to send comfortably across cyberspace. Sending a photo that is one megabyte (mb) or less is just the polite thing to do.

In most cases, you'll use a software program to crop and resize your photo. I use Photoshop, but there are others that work just as well. You probably already have one on your computer. Photoshop allows me to change the resolution. Other programs allow you to crop your photo down to a smaller size without altering the resolution. There are also online photo sites that allow photo alterations. Photoshop.com is one that allows you to crop photos and change resolution. On this site, they use the total resolution (dpi or ppi) to measure a photo. So, they describe a photo that is 2 by 2 inches set at 300 dpi by saying it is 600 x 600, or (2 inches at 300 dots) times (2 inches at 300 dots). Get it?

There are numerous choices out there. Many are free, or come with a product you might already have. Both my computer and digital camera came outfitted with photo management software. You may have to explore and learn in order to be comfortable with your own type of software. Because it is widely used, I will talk about the process using Photoshop here. But, the advice and information regarding dpi, cropping etc. will be the same, whatever program you use.

Setting the correct resolution

The standard resolution for quality printed photos in magazines and newspapers is 300 dpi. Chances are your camera didn't format your photo at 300 dpi. Your number is either higher are lower than 300. You will either increase or decrease to 300 dpi, depending on your camera.

When you are doing this, you want to maintain the total number of dots in your photo. For instance, if you have a 4 by 6 inch photo at 200 dpi, the total number of dots equals (4 x 200) x (6 x 200), or 800 x 1200. If you change the dpi to 300, and the dimensions stay the same, you are adding dots: (4 x 300) x (6 x 300) or 1200 x 1800. Adding dots can make your photo fuzzy, or pixelated, and you don't want to do that.

When you are changing the dpi of your photo, you do not want to "Resample" it. Resample means change the number of dots. So, if your software gives you a choice, make sure the "Resample Image" box is not checked. When this box is not checked, the height and width will change automatically in accordance with changes to the dpi.

The other thing to remember when resizing is this: If your original dpi is lower than 300, the dimensions of you photo should automatically become smaller when you change the dpi to 300. *Repeat: When you increase the dpi, the dimensions decrease.*

This same process works in reverse, if your camera takes photos at a higher resolution than 300 dpi. If your original image is set at 480 dpi and your photo is 7 by 5 inches, that photo size will increase (to about 11 by 8 inches) when you change the resolution to 300 dpi. *Repeat: Decrease the dpi and the dimensions of the photo will increase.*

Cropping

You have your resolution set. Now it is time to crop your photo. When cropping, eliminate as much of the background as possible and focus on your face. I've seen some very striking shots that crop in so close that a portion of the face is actually cropped out. These "partial headshots" can be more effective than one that contains too much background (and not enough you). If you want some great cropping ideas, head to Facebook. There's a plethora of profile photos – most taken by amateurs – that are striking and downright fun.

You'll want to crop so that your image is a square or a vertical rectangle (longer up and down than it is wide – also called "portrait"). The photo that you took is most likely a horizontal rectangle (wider than it is high – also called "landscape"). Most newspapers prefer squares or vertical rectangles.

(There are some photo examples included at the end of this chapter, because you know what they say: A picture is worth a thousand words.)

Sizing

You have the cropping and resolution done, but most likely, the dimensions are still larger than needed. Now it's time to resize your image – or make it smaller. Your software program should allow you the option of seeing and changing the size of your photo under a heading of "Image size" or something similar. This should give you access to the photo dimensions as well as the resolution, or dpi. Or, your program may give you the option of changing the dimensions without accessing the dpi.

Resizing the photo means you are changing the total number of dots. In this case, you are decreasing the number of dots (less dots equals less bytes, or space on your computer). Because you are changing (decreasing) the number of dots, the Resample box (if you have one) should be checked for this step. When you decrease the number of dots, you are resampling or resizing the image. Note: You are decreasing the overall number of dots, but you are not decreasing the dots per inch (dpi). You want to keep that at 300. As a general rule, when working with photos, you never want to increase the number of dots. Increasing dots decreases photo quality. When resizing, only decrease: less dots, not more.

Always constrain the proportions of your photo. What this means is that if you alter the height, the width will automatically change also. This keeps the photo from becoming distorted. To do this make sure that you have the Constrain Proportions box checked. Different software programs use different terminology for this same concept. Microsoft Word uses "Lock Aspect Ratio." Basically, you are looking for wording that indicates that the height will change in proportion to the width, and vice versa. When you have this secured, change the width to 2 inches. For a square photo the other dimension will also change to 2 inches. For a vertical rectangle the height should be about 3 inches. In both cases, the resolution should stay at 300 dpi. When formatted as a jpg, this photo equals about 600 x 600 pixels (for a square) or roughly 355 kilobytes in computer-land. Easily email friendly.

■ ■ ■ ■

In cyberspace, a fast upload is akin to ice cream before supper.

I send a 2 by 2 inch photo, because it is small enough megabyte-wise to make an easy trip through cyberspace via email, while being large enough to give editors enough photo to work with. I'd hate to send a 1 by 1 inch photo, only to have an editor increase its size to 2 by 2 inches and in the process decrease the dpi – and photo quality – by 50 percent. Newsprint has enough challenges without creating one by making your photo too small.

Remember, you are shooting for a cropped photo that is equivalent to 2 by 2 inches at 300 dpi. If your software doesn't let you change the dpi, you can still get a photo that has the correct number of total dots (600 x 600). If your dpi is 150, you'll need a 4 by 4 inch photo to equal the size you need. If you have 400 dpi, you'll only need a 1.5 by 1.5 inch photo. You do the math, depending on your camera and dpi setting. As long as you send a photo that is 600 dots wide and 600 dots high, the design folks at the newspaper can use it without extensive reformatting on their end.

If you aren't able to resize your photo or convert your dpi, you can still know its size before pressing send in your email. Just attach the photo to an email and the size of the file should show up (with my email it is in the lower left corner). If you see a number over one megabyte (1 MB), don't send. You can ask the newspaper editor how large a file he or she will accept. It may be that you can break the rules and still send the photo via email. If all else fails, you can send the old-fashioned way, using an envelope and postage stamp.

Formatting for web use

While newspapers and other print media prefer 300 dpi for quality images, the World Wide Web standard is 72 dpi. You'll want at least a couple of your photos formatted for web use (for use on your website, social networking sites like Facebook and Twitter, writing forums and groups and with your email signature).

Formatting at 72 dpi take up less space (bytes) and in computer-land that means a photo that uploads faster. If you leave your photo at 300 dpi, it will still upload onto your webpage; it will just do so more s-l-o-w-l-y.

Most photo software gives you the option of "formatting for the web," "export for web" or something similar. You don't even have to commit 72 dpi to memory. Just remember to format for the web, because that makes your web pages and other web "stuff" upload faster. In cyberspace, a fast upload is akin to ice cream before supper.

I recommend saving two versions of your web photo: One that is smaller – 2 by 2 inches in size. This can be used for profile shots – Facebook, writing forums, Twitter, etc. A larger shot at about 5 by 5 inches can be used on your own webpage and on other promotional sites that might come up in the future.

Place all your headshots (photos) in one folder within your syndication folder on your computer. You should have one large, full-color shot, another large black and white photo, one formatted for newspapers (about 2 by 2 inches at 300 dpi) and a couple formatted at 72 dpi for the web – one about 2 by 2 inches and a large one that's about 5 by 5 inches.

PHOTO RETAKES

A Review

• Take many photos. One is bound to look good.

• You will want to take your one photo and format it in several different ways, to use in different situations.

• Resolution refers to photo quality. Dpi and ppi refer to resolution. Bytes refer to computer space. Higher resolution equals more bytes.

• Newspapers prefer a resolution of 300 dpi, websites 72 dpi.

• When resizing photos:
If you ***increase*** the dpi, the photo dimensions ***decrease.***
If you ***decrease*** the dpi, the photo dimensions ***increase.***

• Crop in close to your subject (that's you).

• When resizing, constrain the proportions or your photo may become distorted – like looking into a funhouse mirror.

• Aim for a 2 by 2 inch photo at 300 dpi for newspapers. This size is email friendly. Your newspaper editors and publishers will thank you for this!

• Sound complicated? Practice makes perfect!

Photo Samples and Cropping Techniques

Here is the same photo, cropped two different ways. Photo #1 has a professional look. By cropping in closer, in photo #2, you have a more spontaneous, quirky look. Both are attractive shots. You could use either, depending on what you want your headshot to say to readers. I think #1 would be great for a column on fashion, make-up, hairstyles etc., whereas #2 could be a humorous column about funky family life or offbeat observations.

Taken from above, this breaks the have-your-camera-on-level-with-your-subject rule. Another rule broken! Here again, we have just a slight variation on cropping, but see how it changes your shot. In photo #4 you are more able to focus on the face. It's cropped tightly without eliminating features, so it doesn't have the quirky look of photo #2 above. Both are nice, with a natural and earthy feel. Parenting column? Gardening? Take your pick.

Environment Impacts Your Message

These two photos illustrate how environment and accessories can impact your shot. This is the same woman. Does she write a column on fun activities to do with your pet or fun things to do outdoors? Depends on the shot. Your surroundings will help tell your story. What do you want them to say?

When You Need a Suit and Tie…

Sometimes formal is best. This is a very professional looking shot. It is taken nearly head-on, sans fancy, schmancy cropping. Note outdoor, natural background. It provides a backdrop without being distracting. Good shot to use if you are writing a column on legal issues. This guy could be an attorney. In fact, I think he is!

Or are Going for a More Casual Look

This is the same man in photo #7, but with a very different feel, and appeal. I'd go to the guy in photo #7 for banking advice, the one in #8 for parenting tips. Your message impacts your photo. Or at least it should.

A Slice is Nice

This is the shot I currently use. My head is turned slightly to avoid the straight-on shot – no glare from the glasses. I like to think that this shot makes me look like I've got something funny to tell you. I could crop in closer, but I like the effect of having my neck and shoulders in this particular shot. It's a very personal opinion. And, that's a big part of every headshot: personal opinion, which means there is no right or wrong answer. Just your answer. Say "cheese!"

7.

Chapter 7

Finding publication sources
Don't press the "send" button just yet!

An obvious and important step in getting your column printed in newspapers is finding and contacting those papers. But, before you so much as email one editor, you want to make sure you've got a few prerequisites in place. (I'm going to focus on newspapers here, because that is most common and obvious syndication choice – for most columns.)

Email or snail mail? *That is the question.*

Before ever compiling your list of newspapers, decide how you are going to contact them: snail mail or email? For me, this seemed obvious. I do all my correspondence via email. It's handy, convenient and immediate. Also, in this case, it ends up being a whole lot less expensive than snail mail. If you print a hard copy of your query and sample columns, purchase an envelope to put them in and top it all off with first class postage, you are going to spend about a buck for every two queries that you send. I send to about 1,000 newspapers each week – and that only includes six states. By the time I send to all 50 states (my ultimate goal) that 1,000 could be 10,000. I can't imagine having $5,000 a week to spend on self-syndication.

I've heard it whispered on dark street corners that newspaper editors pay more attention to snail mail and your package is more likely to be read if it is sent the old-fashioned way. I question this logic. With snail mail you have to open the envelope, remove the contents, unfold the papers and read. Email requires just a click of the mouse. No pesky envelopes to toss in the garbage. No threat of paper cuts.

In my world, newspaper editors are smart, busy people. They are looking to streamline whenever possible. I think snail mail requires more effort on their part, and I'm looking to make life easier for them.

If you still hesitate about using email, I've got a final nail to put in the coffin of the snail mail debate: word from the editors themselves. I surveyed the newspapers that I work with, and got about 15 responses (so it wasn't the largest of response pools). Still, all of the newspapers – 100 percent – said that their preferred method of communication is through email. That's enough for me. I use email and only email for initial and ongoing contact.

Equipment check

You are going to find publication sources – hopefully lots of them. Before you do, you want to make sure that your system can handle the job. (And that you know your system well enough to help it handle the job.)

It's preferable to have high-speed Internet. If you have dial-up and are able to upgrade, I'd advise it. As you come to send and receive hundreds or thousands of emails, speed will become a factor.

Are you happy with your email service provider? If you are thinking about a change six months down the road, you might want to take care of that now. Once you start syndicating and distributing your email out there for the world to see, it will be much harder to change that email without losing editors and readers.

Most email providers allow you to have at least a couple of email accounts (names). Look into setting one up just for your syndicated emails. That way, when you get messages back from editors, they all go into one place and you don't have to sort through your other "regular" emails from Aunt Tilly and that special sale announcement from the department store.

How's your address book? Are you comfortable working in it? Do you find it easy to access information? What kind of information can you include with addresses? Do you know how to move and change information? Set up folders? Spend a little time familiarizing yourself with how your address book works. Plan, ahead of time, how you will organize your information. (More on that later.)

Locating newspapers

Finding and compiling your information

There are a number of ways you can find newspaper email addresses. I found online services that provide email and snail mail addresses for a fee. Mondo Times is one. Although they charge a fee for email addresses, just about everything else including web addresses, circulation information and names of editors, is free. I didn't want to pay a fee, so I took the do-it-yourself thing to a whole new level and found the addresses myself. The best way to do this varies state by state. (I never said this was going to be easy.)

I tackle a state at a time. I start with a Google search for an individual state's newspaper association – for instance, Minnesota Newspaper Association (www.mna.org). Each state seems to have a similar site. If you find one that doesn't, you can go to a site like Mondo and work outward from there. (Contact websites for this are in the last chapter.)

Within this newspaper association site, you can often access a listing of newspapers, including contact names, circulation, phone numbers and email addresses. Now we enter the cut and paste portion of the show.

You will become one with your address book during this part of the syndication process. I cut and paste names, emails and circulation information into my addresses. This avoids typos; keyboard accuracy is not my forte. Type in the name of the state in the memo section as well. As your distribution grows, and you need to find a particular address or newspaper, having the state information included makes locating its particular state folder easier. You'll need this information if you want to move the address to a different folder – say your "yes" group.

Include circulation information (if available) in the memo section so that later, when the newspaper contacts you about running your column, you will know how happy your happy dance should be. If the newspaper is part of a larger conglomerate, list that in the comments section as well. If you get published in one paper of "US Papers Inc." maybe you can use that to your advantage and develop a message to approach other newspapers within the parent company. It also helps you to keep track of whom you are sending your information to within the conglomerate.

Large newspaper conglomerates

When I am dealing with a larger company, I try to keep track of whom I am sending email to within that company. I do not want to send five emails to the same person – even though that person may serve as publisher or editor to five papers. I want as many eyes as possible to see my columns. If one person within the conglomerate of US Papers Inc.

I cut and paste names, emails and circulation information into my address book. This avoids typos; keyboard accuracy is not my forte.

sees my column, I have one chance that it will be noticed and published. If I send to five decision-makers within that same company, I've increased my chances for success by five times.

In addition, sending the same email five times to the same email address (i.e. person) makes me look unorganized – like I don't know what I am doing or to whom I am sending email. Not only that, but receiving those five emails would be annoying.

Q: Who is this woman who keeps filling up my inbox?
A: Who cares?

So, if Joe Newsy serves as publisher for six papers, I send to his editors at five. I may send one email to him. I do my best to keep track of this, but again, we aren't dealing in science, we are dealing in syndication. If Joe Newsy happens to get two emails from me, so be it. I do my best to avoid this, however, and I recommend that you do the same.

Identifying the folks who work at multiple papers can be accomplished by using the search feature within your address book. This makes the information that you place in the comments section important. You can't be expected to remember everyone's name – especially when you are dealing with thousands of them. This is why you need your notes!

Sometimes, the emails listed at the newspaper association site are generic and not addressed to a specific person. For instance, an address of: news@newspaper.com might be listed, but the personal address of the editor, Joe Smith, is: Jsmith@newspaper.com. I think using the personal address is preferred; your email is more likely to get to John Smith if you use his specific address; so if you can find it, use it.

Often, that means clicking on a newspaper's website and doing a little detective work. I've gotten good at this. When you are on a homepage, look for buttons (or places to click) labeled with words like "Contact Us," "Our Staff," "Directory" or "Email Us." They are often around the periphery of the page. Newspapers vary greatly in regard to how easy they make it for you to email their editors or publishers. Sometimes email addresses are right there for the taking; other times they are embedded three or four clicks into the page.

If I've spent more than a few minutes on one newspaper, I relent and use the generic address. I try to "process" a newspaper – that is, enter its information into my address book within a minute or two. If all the information is at the newspaper association site and I don't have to click on a newspaper's website, I can do a couple a minute. In the best circumstance, I can enter 60-plus newspapers into my address book in an hour. For a state with 200 newspapers, we're looking at a time commitment of three hours.

I have found a number of states that do not list email addresses on their newspaper association website. In these cases I have to access Mondo Times and click on each individual newspaper website and hunt until I find email addresses. It takes a long time (8 hours for 160 addresses!). At first I thought this was a complete bummer. But, I have since found that the email addresses listed on a newspaper's own website are much more likely to be accurate than email addresses found on the newspaper association website. I am also more likely to find the personal email information, versus the generic information that is often listed on a state's newspaper association site.

For instance, I recently processed one state where the information was not available from the newspaper association site. I accessed each individual newspaper website through Mondo Times and found addresses that way. Of the 160 email addresses that I found, only two were wrong.

In contrast, I processed a different state where the information on email addresses was listed at their state newspaper association website. I cut and copied addresses directly from the site, bypassing individual newspaper websites (for the most part). On email day, I sent off 160 messages, only to have 38 returned with a message that there was an error with the email address. It took me about two hours to make my way through the error messages and get the correct addresses listed in my files.

The message, I guess, is that maybe there is no easy way to compile hundreds or thousands of email addresses. If they are easily accessible from one website, chances are you will find more errors. If you have to traverse, website by website, painstakingly seeking individual addresses, you will spend more time initially, but your accuracy will improve significantly. Nothing about compiling addresses is fun – until one editor replies with a positive comment regarding your columns!

Whom to send to?

If you are like me, this phase provides you with a dilemma. Whose name do you file in your address book – publisher or editor (or someone else)? I haven't figured this one out yet. If the paper is really huge, I figure the publisher isn't hands-on for daily decisions and I use the address for the editor.

When it comes to email, I have found that editor addresses are more likely to be correct. In some cases, a publisher does not maintain an email at every newspaper and instead has an email that (I'm assuming) he or she answers from corporate headquarters, or maybe one of the seven newspapers for which he or she serves as publisher. I want to reach a real, live person at each newspaper. So, with that line of thinking, it might be better to seek out editors.

On the other hand, editors are busy with the day-to-day workings of a newspaper. Sometimes they may not have time to consider, much less read, a new column submission. Publishers may look at things a little differently. They are in the business of publishing a profitable newspaper. A really great column – and its sales-potential – might catch a publisher's eye. I have had situations where an editor overlooked my column until prompted to review it by the publisher. In other words, just when I think I have it figured out, I figure that I don't.

Sometimes I base my decision on a name. If a particular name sounds good to me, I send to that address. This is a highly scientific and fact-based method. It is only recommended for people who got a C+ or better in chemistry in high school. Use at your own risk.

Editor or publisher? I don't think there is a right answer. Maybe, in certain situations, you want to send to both. Mouse clicks are cheap. You could send to the editor for a certain amount of time (three to six months) and then, if you haven't had a response, switch to the publisher.

Depending on your topic, your column may fit best in a certain section of the newspaper. The obvious choice for syndicated work is the opinion page, but other options might be the entertainment, editorial, lifestyle, home or food sections. Keep this in mind when you are researching email addresses, especially for larger newspapers that employ editors for each section of their paper. You will want to pick the email address for the editor working most closely to your column's topic.

The good news is that, for the most part, newspaper folks are some of the best around. They will be more than forgiving if your email ends up in the wrong cyber mailbox. In most cases, they will forward your message to the appropriate person within their particular organization.

Organizing your address book

You might start out being published in just one paper, but if you want to see that grow, your address book is going to be brimming with names and newspapers – thousands of them. Managing that many addresses requires a system. I organize addresses by state.

When compiling my initial list, all addresses for one state go into one folder (for instance "Minnesota"). After contact begins, that one folder grows into three: the original folder, one for newspapers that can use the column and one for the papers that have no known email address, bad email addresses or that request to be taken off my mailing list.

Because my address book organizes folders alphabetically, and because I want to keep my groups (the yes's, no's and original folders) grouped together, I label the "yes" folders starting with "AA" – for instance "AA Slices MN." This puts them together at the top of my address book. The "no" folders are labeled starting with "ZZ" – "ZZ no email no thanks MN." The original folders stay the same, without any double letter prefix – "Minnesota," placing them in the middle of my address list. Having each group together makes it much easier to send the column. I don't have to search for the "yes" group; they are all huddled together at the top of my address book.

Keeping the addresses in folders serves another purpose. It keeps your distribution list confidential. Newspapers receiving my columns know that I am sending to Minnesota and Iowa, but they don't know which newspapers I am sending to within those states. Keeping everyone's email addresses confidential is respectful and professional.

Spend some time thinking about how you want to list the names of individual newspapers within your address book. The official moniker of many papers starts with the word "The," as in "The New York Times," and "The Washington Post." You'll find yourself wading through one "The" after another if you simply type in the name of the newspaper and let it go

Include circulation information in the memo section of your addresses so that later, when the newspaper contacts you about running your column, you will know how happy your happy dance should be.

at that. You could leave out common words, like "the," but then you'd have to remember – or have a way of keeping track of – your edits. I record each newspaper name as written (including the common words like the), but I begin each entry with the name of the town or city where the newspaper is located. If the name of the town or city is duplicated in the newspaper name, it is not typed in a second time. For instance, The Park Rapids Enterprise is recorded as "Park Rapids, The Enterprise," The Cloquet Pine Journal becomes "Cloquet, The Pine Journal."

Seems like duh common sense when you see it laid out like I just did, but it took me a couple hundred addresses (and quite a bit of searching for a particular newspaper) to come up with my simplistic and logical solution.

Again, include more information – versus less – in the comments section of each address entry. If you are sending to the editor, cut and paste the name and email information for the publisher, if it is available. Include information on circulation, parent company, website, phone number etc. If in doubt, cut and paste. You'll likely thank yourself later.

8.

Chapter 8

Approaching your sources
The email package

You've got your columns and your addresses. You are on the brink. Time to compile information to send in your initial email to newspapers. What exactly should you include in this all-important introductory email?

In the initial query, I include a letter and three sample columns. Historically, columnists have been advised to send at least four and as many as six sample columns. I figure that's more than any editor will need or want to read initially – especially when I will follow up my first email with a new column each week. I try to keep everything about my initial contact as brief as possible, while still giving all the information that is needed.

I cut and paste everything into the body of the email. Attachments are often hostile entities in the email world. Never send them unless requested to do so. I use a regular font – Arial or Helvetica. I like sans serif, but Times is okay, too.

Make sure your query is grammatically correct. Check and then double check for spelling errors. If you edit so much as one word, re-read the entire email again to make sure it is correct and without errors. DO NOT USE EXCESSIVE CAPITAL LETTERS OR PUNCTUATION!!! It makes readers feel like you are shouting. This is your one and only chance to make that grand first impression. You don't want to blow it by sending an email that is anything other than perfect.

What do editors and publishers want?

Before you can compose your query letter, it helps to understand the perspectives of editors and publishers. Why should they care about you or your syndicated column? Quite simply, they will care if it benefits them in some way. Will you increase circulation? Sales? Readership? Will you decrease the editor's workload? How do you know?

I surveyed some of the papers that use my column regarding their preferences and what they look for when considering a column for publication. The good news is that a majority of papers (about 75 percent) use submitted columns regularly – from once a month to once a week. When deciding to publish a column, the most important factor for just about every paper was subject matter. Newspapers are looking for a topic that is of interest to readers – something pertinent, entertaining and appealing to the masses.

Three answers tied for second place. They were: cost, quality of writing and space considerations. I discussed cost in chapter five.

Editors are looking for grammatically correct copy that needs little or no editing and is ready to print as sent by the columnist. Quality is something that you'll have to prove over time. When you send your initial query with three columns, you'll want to make sure they are high-quality writing, but that isn't going to be enough for the majority of editors. They will want to see you produce quality material consistently week after week.

More than a few editors mentioned they prefer shorter columns because they are easier to place. The mantra? Less is more. I try to keep mine between 500 and 800 words.

Your goal is to make life easier for overworked editors by giving them a valuable piece of copy that easily slips into their paper and will be well-liked by readers.

Composing the query letter

Ah, the letter. It is tempting to include a three-page bio about your success in the writing world. Don't. Keep your note short, sweet and to the point. You may have the most impressive resume on the planet, but the only thing that an editor is interested in (you hope) is your column.

In my survey of newspaper editors, the number one reason for considering a column for publication was appeal to readers. I want editors to know that my column is of interest to readers, but I do not want to come across as a know-it-all who is telling the editor what to do. It's a gray area. Proceed carefully. You want to get your message across without alienating anyone named Editor.

Use the query letter to put your name and the name of your column in front of the editor's face. Remember he or she will have to see this information at least a few times before committing it to memory.

You'll want to touch on payment; but keep this brief. Don't spend half your query letter with money talk. It would be a big turn-off from an editor's perspective. I touch on money (mention it at least!), but keep it loose. I don't want to lose an editor before he or she has had the chance to even read one of my columns.

My letters vary from state to state – I get bored with the same old, same old – but they average around 300 words. I keep them short and sweet, because I value the time of newspaper editors. Sending a brief letter shows this.

It goes without saying (although I'll say it here) that your letter needs to be grammatically correct and without typos or spelling errors. Any error,

FOR INSTANCE

The initial query letter

Step by step. Paragraph by paragraph.

Your intro letter, while brief, is important. It needs to communicate certain key elements with just a few sentences. Here's what I do:

First paragraph - *name recognition*

Column name, my name, my brief bio/history along with that of the column. Two sentences.

Second paragraph - *the basic facts*

What I propose to do and how that benefits the editor.
Type of column, length, how often I will send.
Another two sentences.

Third paragraph - *my requests*

That they email when using the column and include my bio at the end. I touch on money stuff, but keep this loose.
Two or three sentences.

Fourth paragraph - *try it, you'll like it!*

Offer a test drive. "I've cut and pasted three sample columns below. Please use them in your paper, free of charge, and see what your readers think." I offer to send a photo to use as a header. Finally, I thank them for their time and consideration.

'Nuff said.

no matter how minor, can cause an editor to form an initial negative impression. Nothing but perfection will do.

Emailing – finally!

I want to set myself up as responsible and competent. I want newspapers to rely on me. This means emailing at a consistent time each week. My time is Monday mornings. It seemed like an obvious choice. I let papers know that if they haven't heard from me by noon on Monday, they can feel free to email me because something has gone wrong in cyberspace. (And this does happen.)

This consistent schedule begins with my initial email. It always goes out on Monday morning. If I have a new group of addresses ready to go on Thursday, they wait until the next Monday.

When completing my first email communication to papers, I send each note individually (no group emails) so I can include the name of the editor or publisher in the salutation. Is this overkill? Maybe. But maybe not, and you only get one chance to make a first impression. This extra step adds time into the initial mailing process, but I'm doing everything I can to do things right and get noticed by the good folks at the newspaper.

Mailing shortcuts

When you send out multiple emails that contain the same information, there are ways to streamline the process. I like to compose everything in

It might not seem like much at first, but by streamlining the process, you are saving yourself tens, if not hundreds, of mouse clicks.

my word processing program. I write the query and then cut and paste the three columns (including my bio information at the end of each column) below the letter. Then, I proofread everything – carefully – checking for errors and correcting any that I find.

Next I cut and paste the entire Word document into my email. I recheck the query letter and columns to make sure that my formatting didn't change during the cut and paste process. Then I cut and paste my email signature. I move it from the bottom of my very lengthy document and place it between my query letter and the first sample column. I recheck everything again to make sure spacing and formatting look spot on.

When I have everything looking great, I select all and copy the entire email. I save the email into my drafts. Next, I open a new email (to send), delete my email signature (if it automatically appears on my blank email) and paste the query and column into the new email. I save that into my drafts. I repeat. If I am sending 25 emails, I do this 25 times: Click to send new email. Click to paste the information into the email. Click to save to drafts. Repeat.

I now have all the bodies of my emails completed. Next I streamline typing into the subject line. I only want to type my subject line once. I open one email draft. I type my information into the subject line: "Jill Pertler, Slices of Life, column submission." Then I highlight and copy the text from my subject line.

I open my address book and click on the first address that I want to access. I go into the body of my email and type a salutation using the recipient's first name, if possible. Then I send.

I go into my drafts; open a second of my emails. I click on the subject line and paste in the subject. Next I click on the second address in my list, include a salutation and press send. And so on.

It might not seem like much at first, but by streamlining the process, you are saving yourself tens if not hundreds of mouse clicks and that equals time saved – always a good thing. I find I can complete a first mailing of about 250 addresses in about two hours. Your fingers might be even quicker than mine.

The all-important subject line:
Jill Pertler, Slices of Life, column submission

Don't underestimate the importance of the wording in your subject line. It should not be an afterthought. You want to be brief. You want the editor to see the information you've chosen. If possible, you want to include the name of your column and your own name. Why? The average person (a.k.a. editor) has to see the same piece of information from five to eight times (sometimes more) before he or she commits it to memory. You are using your subject line to make up for one of those times – and you are tying your name to the name of your column. Unless you are already famous, you'll want to do whatever you can to improve your own name recognition, and to have it associated with the name of your column. If you can get the editor to open your email and see your name and column title again, you're two down with a few more to go.

I also include the words "column submission." They are obvious and to-the-point. I want to be up-front and honest with editors. I don't want to trick them into opening my email with some cryptic phrase. I am sending a column submission – and proud of it!

Jill Pertler, Slices of Life, column submission says what I want it to say and accomplishes my goals at the same time.

Once I have established relationships with newspapers, I revise the subject line to include a short description and word count: Jill Pertler, Slices of Life, texting teens, 711 wds.

Notes on the salutation

Offering a first-name salutation is often a good idea, but there are some cases where I leave it out. John, Mary, Steve and Laura are all people I'll address in the salutation, because their names leave little room for questions. But, if I can't get a name right, sometimes it's best to leave it out. If a person is named "Richard," for instance, do I address the email to Dick? Rich? Rick? Richard? I believe that if someone known as "Rick" gets an email addressed to "Dick," the salutation does more to say "Hey, I don't know you from Adam," than a simple "Hello" without any name attached. My husband's given name is "Thomas." Does he go by Thomas, Tommy or Tom? Neither. He uses Thom, and an email or any correspondence addressed to Tom (without the "h") is an immediate tip-off that the sender hasn't done his or her homework. Because there are gray areas when it comes to names, there are some instances where I leave out the personalization and stick with an unadorned "Hello."

Again, my system is far from scientific. But, every step of the way, I try to put myself in an editor's shoes and do whatever it takes to be respectful and make life easier for him or her. Getting someone's name wrong is not respectful. In fact, it could be irritating. Irritating an editor is exactly what I don't want to do.

The initial mailing

I talk about mailing to 200-plus addresses in one morning, but my first group of emails was much smaller than that. I know you are chomping at the bit to get started, but I recommend starting out gradually – with 10 to 25 addresses. Approach those papers and send, send, send your information each week. If you have problems or bugs to work out (believe me, there will be bugs) you can do so on a small scale. If there are changes that you find you need to make in your address book, it's much easier to do so with 25 addresses versus 250 or 2,500.

As your process becomes seamless and smooth, add 25 more addresses. I think you'll find adding the second 25 comes much easier than the first 25. From there you can increase exponentially. Two hundred (or more) at a time.

9.

Chapter 9

Relationship building after you press "send"
The yes's, no's and everyone else

After you hit the send button, the replies will start rolling in. These first emails will not be offers to publish your column; so don't be disappointed. Those offers take a little time – at least long enough for the editor to read your sample columns! The first email responses will likely be error messages due to bad email addresses, typos etc. In one mailing of 260 addresses, I received 16 error emails (six percent). Of these failures, I was able to research (by going to each newspaper's website) and find the correct address for 12 of the 16 within about 30 minutes time.

Within the next 24 hours, I heard from 14 more papers (about five percent). Half of these were "no's." One paper didn't have money in its budget. Six didn't have room or only used local columnists. One was an out-of office reply.

Now for the good news: two newspapers requested that I send my samples as an attachment. And for the really good news: three papers replied with a "yes!"

What to do with the no's

When a newspaper asks to be taken off your distribution list, do so graciously and immediately. Move the address into your "no thanks" folder for that state, delete it from its state folder (so no more emails get sent to that address) but don't delete it from your address book. You may want to send them a column once or twice a year, just to let them know what they are missing. When you do, you will want to personalize the email so they know they aren't erroneously back on your list. Restate your terms. Newspaper editors and publishers change all the time, so it's worth a shot to revisit.

Don't feel rejected. It is okay. I used to be afraid to open emails from newspapers because I didn't know if they would be a "yes" or a "no." You will get some of both, which is way more than you'd get if you never sent your columns out at all.

When I get a "no," I may respond back – usually when an editor makes positive comments about my writing. I give a short, kind reply wishing the editor well. If I get a terse "REMOVE" request, I don't reply. I figure the editor is very busy and probably won't appreciate another interruption from me. Replying (or not) depends on each individual circumstance and is your call. I always try to do what would seem the most polite and considerate from the editor's perspective.

What to do with the yes's

Newspapers that indicate they will print your column get the kid glove treatment. They go into their own address book file, so you can personalize the email each week to acknowledge your appreciation of working together with them. Double-check the name of the person returning your emails. You may have the publisher, Joe Smith, in your files, but the general manager, Karen Johnson, is your email contact. Address your emails to Karen. It is the respectful thing to do if you are corresponding with her. Likewise, if you sent your original email to Josh R. Nelson and the reply comes back from "J.R.," make the revision in your address book. The key here? Paying a little attention shows a lot of respect.

When you get a yes, respond faster than immediately. Show the newspaper that you are on the ball and at your computer able to communicate at a moment's notice.

Cyberspace can do funny things when you cut and paste your column into the body of an email. Most editors just deal with this and do the reformatting on their end. There are a few, however, that prefer to receive columns as an attachment. Ask each paper about its preference and send accordingly. This will require another folder in your address book: one for the newspapers that Want Attachments.

Finally, email a headshot that the editor can use with the column.

Now is the time to firm up payment. Does the editor prefer that you send an invoice each month, or will he or she keep track of when columns run and send payment accordingly? Provide your payment address.

Often an editor brings up the subject of payment. Sometimes he asks where he should send your check, or inquires about your rates. This makes it easy to jump into a dialogue regarding fees. Other editors forget or don't ask about payment and leave it to you to broach the subject. At first, this made me nervous. What if they rejected me because I asked to be paid? Eek.

I still get a little nervous when I have to initiate the subject of payment. It's not my favorite part of the job. But, if I want more of those paychecks, it has to get done.

When an editor (or publisher) fails to mention payment, I ask if they have money in their budget to pay columnists. I tell them that I am thankful they are able to find space for my words, but that I also have to pay for the groceries. I find they are honest, and understanding. We talk money and so far it's always resulted in a positive working relationship.

Asking about payment, reminds editors that you should be paid. However, you'll still need to have an answer ready for those papers that are not willing or able to pay you. Your answer is a personal one based on your unique situation.

Organizing information when newspapers respond positively to your email

When you hear back with a "yes," from a newspaper, there are a number of pieces of information that you'll want track. You'll need a system. Here's how I do it:

I organize my communications based on individual states. Minnesota has its own file. Wisconsin. Iowa. You get the picture. On my hard drive, I have a folder labeled "Syndication." Within that folder, I have a folder for each state. Within each state folder I have a file for the emails I send and receive to papers within that state. (This does not include my weekly emails sent with the column; they are located elsewhere. More on that later.)

When I receive an email from a newspaper regarding publishing my column, I follow a four-step procedure for recording the information:

Step one: I cut and paste the email from the newspaper into the corresponding state file. I include the date and any response that I may have sent to the email. Newer emails go on top of older ones, so I can locate a specific correspondence based on date, if needed.

Step two: I have another file, within the Syndication folder, labeled "Newspapers printed." This file contains a list of all the newspapers that carry my column. It is organized alphabetically by (you guessed it) state. Within this list, I include: the name of the paper, the date they contacted me about publishing the column, the circulation of the paper, the name of my contact at the paper and payment information.

Within this file, I keep track of the number of papers I am printed in within each state and cumulatively. I also keep track of circulation – total and state by state.

Step three: I go to my address book and find the newspaper in question. In the comments section I note the date and contact person (changing the contact name if needed). I then take the address and put it in my "yes" directory for the corresponding state: "AA Slices MN," and remove the address from the generic state directory: "Minnesota."

Step four: I go into my spreadsheet, where I have newspapers organized by state. I record the name of the newspaper, start date for publication, contact person and payment information. Later I will record when invoices are sent and checks received. This spreadsheet may sound a lot like the file described in step two where I list all newspapers

FOR INSTANCE

The 4-step process for organizing your yes's

Step 1
Keep track of emails sent and received in a state-specific file.

Step 2
Include newspaper name and other pertinent information in a list of all newspapers that are printing your column.

Step 3
Move address to "yes" folder in your address book.

Step 4
Record billing information in your spreadsheet.

that print my column. There is some overlap, but each file is useful to me in different ways. I need the spreadsheet to keep track of money coming in (and bills sent). I use the Word file listing the newspapers to keep track of circulation numbers. Because I started out gradually, I didn't need the spreadsheet right away. So, I had the circulation file set up, and then developed a need for a way to keep track of the monetary end of things.

What to do with everyone else

All other papers stay on your mailing list. The addresses stay in their own state folder and they are all seen as potentials. Keep sending. Keep sending. Keep sending. Like a patient fisherperson, you are waiting for them to take the bait. Every Monday morning, like clockwork, hit that send button.

I have found that most newspapers won't respond after the initial contact. Why should they? They don't know me; they don't know my work. They don't know that I am responsible and can meet deadlines. They may have enough copy that week, and the week after that. But, there will come a time when they are in need of good, quality copy. When this time comes, I want to be the first person/writer that comes to mind:

I used to be afraid to open emails from newspapers because I didn't know if they would be a "yes," or a "no." You will get some of both, which is way more than you'd get if you never sent your columns out at all.

Hey, there's that writer from Minnesota who sends us those funny columns every week. Maybe we can give her a try.

I like to include a short – one to two-sentence – note with my columns each week. I try to connect it to my column if I can. It's one more way to build relationships – to personalize my email and take it from general and generic to personal and personable. An editor is more likely to want to work with you if he or she feels you have an established relationship.

For instance, one week I wrote a rather serious piece on the fact that I am in the "sandwich years;" I have kids young enough to need me and parents old enough to need me, leaving me sandwiched in the middle. Because this was a serious column, I wanted my note to be a little more lighthearted, so I wrote:

"There are lots of us who are sandwiched. I like to think of myself as a turkey with pepper jack: basically healthy, but with a little spicy kick thrown in for good measure. Being sandwiched often feels serious, because it is. But, if you can't find something to laugh at you'll go crazy. And that's the truth."

By including a short email, I am again drawing the editor's attention to my name. Repeat the mantra: Name recognition will help me gain publication sources in the long run.

> *Q: Jill who?*
> *A: Isn't she the one who writes those columns about deli meats?*

Always remind papers (that haven't yet published your column) to email you if they can use it. A short, polite sentence at the end of your email is all it takes: "Please drop a line if you can use this." It's brief, but you do need that short, sweet sentence to encourage editors to communicate so you can keep track of your circulation and publication information.

I mentioned earlier that editors will be more likely to publish your column if it benefits them. The same goes for communication and dropping you that email you so desire. If you have a website (and you should) you can offer to post a link to a newspaper's website when they email to let you know they've published your column online. This gives newspapers an incentive to publish your column, *and* to communicate with you about their actions. You get the information. They get more web hits. It's a good deal all-around.

About once every six weeks or so, you can compose a more sales-heavy email. Pitch your column in a more direct way. You might want to let editors know that five newspapers have started publishing your column in the last month. Do they want to give you a try as well? If you've received positive feedback from an editor or publisher, you could include that in your pitch. Keep it short and sweet, however. You want to remind them that you are out there, but you don't want to be a pest.

Alignment of the stars

There are a number of things – besides name recognition – that have to happen before the stars can align causing an editor to decide to publish your well-written, fiendishly funny, unique and irresistible column. First, he or she has to find the time to actually read your words. Don't laugh. Editors are busy people with lots of material to read before their current issue goes to press. It is likely that your column will not be read within minutes or even hours (or days) of the editor first receiving your email.

After an editor does read your column – and likes it – he or she will most likely want a second (and third) opinion. What do others at the paper think of your ideas? Hopefully, they love them. Let's imagine everyone at the paper loves your advice column, except for one thing: they already have an advice columnist. And the paper is currently full.

But low and behold, four months pass and the advice columnist runs off with a professional bear hunter from Alaska, freeing up some space in the newspaper. When that space opens up, whom will the editor think of? Your consistent quality, errorless delivery and relationship building efforts will put you tops on an editor's list. That's right where you want to be.

Often an editor will offer a "trial" run. They want to see what readers think of your work. In my experience, a "trial" or "I'm going to print you this week," is likely to turn into a regular gig. When an editor sees how easy it is to cut and paste your columns into the paper, and when reader response is positive, he or she would be unwise to not print your good words.

So far, I've found that within about six months of sending my column, I will hear back with favorable responses from about 10 percent of newspapers. (Patience is a virtue. Or so I keep telling myself.) If I send to 250, I can expect to be published in 25 within six months. Your numbers may be different, depending on your subject matter and quality of writing, to name just a couple of variables. My main point in giving you these statistics is to let you know that you probably will not hear back from the majority of your sources. This is no reflection on the quality of your work. It's the nature of the business.

Newspapers stay on my mailing list unless they request to be removed. That means forever. They haven't told me to go away, so I

You probably will not hear back from the majority of your sources. This is no reflection on the quality of your work. It's the nature of the business.

don't; and once I have them in my address book, it costs no money or extra time to click my mouse and send them a column each week. Each newspaper is a potential customer waiting for the right circumstances to use my services. Maybe a columnist leaves. Maybe the paper expands. Maybe they get a new editor... or publisher. Whatever, I want to be there in the front of the line to capitalize on columnist possibilities when they do happen.

Email error messages and other automated replies

Each week, I get a few emails returned with error messages attached. Sometimes the problem is as simple as an editor's mailbox being full and I get a message that reads something like: *User mailbox exceeds allowed size* or *User over quota*. When this happens, I make a note of the error message in the comments section of the address listing in my address book. Then, I wait a few hours and resend the email. I want to give the editor in question time to get into the office, check on emails and empty out his or her email box.

Other messages such as: *Action failed, Illegal or unknown address, User unknown, Host or domain name not found, Recipient unknown* or *Name service error* indicate a problem with the email address. Sometimes addresses change. Sometimes newspapers change their email security settings. When I get one of these messages, I note it in the comments section of my address listing for that newspaper. The first time I get a failure message, I try to do a little website research to find the correct or updated address. I am successful about half the time. If I can't find a new address, I wait a day and retry the address that gave me the error message (just in case something was weird with cyberspace the first time I sent it). If it comes back again as an error, I move the address to my "no email, no thanks" folder. When I do find a new address I resend the column using it. If it comes back returned, I re-try the first address. If I fail again, I remove the address to my "no thanks" file.

Out of office replies come back when someone is on vacation or out of the office. If I get one of these messages from a newspaper that regularly prints my column, I double check with another person at the paper to make sure they received the column successfully. If an out of office reply comes from another paper (one that doesn't carry my column) I ignore it and send a new column the next week.

Small newspapers vs. large ones

When I started the self-syndication process, I had visions of making it to the big time by getting my column into larger newspapers (circulation 100,000 or more). For the most part, that hasn't happened. Larger papers have columnists on staff, so they don't have as much need for my services. In addition, I think the larger papers would lean toward using a traditionally syndicated columnist (versus a self-syndicated "beginner" like myself).

I've really enjoyed getting to know the editors of small town newspapers. Just like big-city editors, they appreciate good writing. Many times they don't have a columnist on staff, nor do they have time to write a column themselves, so my words are a welcome addition to their paper.

I still send my columns to the larger papers, and I'd still like the chance to get a run in a few of them. But, until that happens – and even after it does – I've come to value the small town papers and the exposure and readers they provide.

10.

Chapter 10

The business end: *Keeping track of and organizing your information*

I learned long ago that my memory is far from perfect, so I keep track of everything.

Columns published

My columns – all of 'em – are stored on my hard drive in a folder labeled columns published. Within this folder are folders labeled by year – 2009, 2010, etc. Each week, I save my columns using first the date (021510) followed by a descriptive title like: "Cell phones body parts" For: 021510 Cell phones body parts. Each of these files then goes into the corresponding year's folder

Every so often I should (wish I did it more often) back up my files onto a portable hard drive. They can also go on a flash drive. The more back up the better – monthly would be good, weekly preferable. Make it part of your routine. (You can even get software to do this for you automatically.)

I also recommend printing out a hard copy of each column and filing it in a three-ring binder. You'll have an instant "book," and something to read on cold dark nights.

I also have a file that lists just the column titles in chronological order. This is useful when I'm trying to remember when I last wrote to complain about the garbage company, or my husband's preoccupation with the TV remote control.

Praise

What a fun thing to track! I have a file just for the positive comments I receive regarding my columns. I keep them in chronological order, making sure to include the date as well as the full name of the person dishing out said compliment. Include these bits of praise on your website – sort of as a running log of testimonials. You can also include a select few in promo materials that you create. If you receive a particularly good one, use it in one of your weekly emails to the newspapers that haven't yet responded to your tantalizing column offers.

If nothing more, they are just fun to read – especially after a rejection or especially hard day.

Email

I've described some of my record-keeping practices in the previous chapter. To recap, I keep a log of emails received from newspapers that want to run my column. In this log, I include my own reply emails. They are organized according to state. Each state has its own Word file. Within each file, the emails are organized in chronological order (always include the date with each email), with the newer emails pasted above the previous ones. I keep the emails from each individual newspaper grouped together, so I can easily follow a thread of communication from a certain editor.

In addition to this, I keep one file that contains the emails I send each week with my column. I haven't had to access this file often, but it doesn't take more than a moment to cut and paste my message to newspapers. If needed, I can see if I am being redundant, or if a question comes up, I can access my exact words and know precisely what I emailed off when I clicked my mouse. Better safe than sorry.

Invoicing

You'll need a method to keep track of monetary transactions. That is, invoices you send and checks you receive. I recommend sending invoices out once a month (at the beginning of the month seems logical).

Information to include with an invoice:

- The fact that this is an invoice
- The date
- The name of your column
- Your name and contact number
- Name of the client/newspaper you are billing
- Contact person at the newspaper
- Contact information (email, phone and/or physical address)
- Description of the work being billed
- Amount billed
- Some sort of legal statement about interest accruing on unpaid balances
- **Where to send the check!**
- A *thanks for your business* is always a nice touch

A copy of a sample invoice is included at the end of this chapter.

I've found that some newspapers prefer quarterly invoices. That works, too. Just make sure you have a method of keeping track of who gets what and when.

I have my information organized in a spreadsheet, but I am far from an expert in this area. Just know that you should record when you invoice, how much you invoice for and when you are paid for that invoice.

Come up with (a.k.a design) one "master" invoice that you can fill in the blanks for various newspapers each month. I have fancy graphic design software programs (because of my other marketing business) so I have a slick-looking invoice that I send. I do this via email, using a pdf file.

That is, I create my invoice in my graphics program and export as a pdf file. You could do the same thing with a jpeg if you have that capability. Or, you can use a simple Word file and send it as is. Just about everyone has Microsoft Word and can open a Word document (even a Mac user, like me!). Because these are newspapers that I work and communicate with regularly, I feel a sort of camaraderie with them. This allows me to break my initial rule (another rule broken) and send the invoice as an attachment. If you don't want to send an attachment, you can cut and paste your information from Word directly into the body of your email.

Keeping track of all the paychecks you receive is important. Having all your information in one place on one spreadsheet will be useful come tax time.

Where your column is (really) printed

The importance of Googling and Alerts

You have a list of all the newspapers that print your column – or at least you have the newspapers that have told you they are printing your column. And, despite your diligence of sending happy emails with a request that papers contact you if they can use your column, sometimes newspapers print your column, but don't contact you. You can find them (at least some of them) by doing a Google search of your own name. It's kind of fun, to see your name and your columns pop up on the screen. Over time, I've watched the hits for my name go from one page, to three, to seven and now more than a dozen as my column has grown and branched out to more and more papers.

As your column (and your popularity) grows, you may want to set up a Google Alert using your name. What this does is provide you with an email message that includes all sightings of your name (or name of your column or whatever you alert Google to alert you about). You can receive updates as they happen, once a day or once a week. All it takes is registering with Google.

When you do a regular Google search, you'll see familiar names – of the newspapers you are working with. But, there will be the occasional spotting of a newspaper that is printing your column without communicating this with you.

Are you outraged? Upset? Why would someone take your column and use it without showing you the courtesy of dropping an email (and paycheck)?

Before you jump to any conclusions, realize that this situation does happen – more often than you'd imagine. This can happen for a number of (legitimate) reasons:

- The editor is busy. She intends to contact you, but just doesn't get to it.
- The editor doesn't realize he is supposed to contact you.
- The editor thinks the publisher has contacted you. The publisher thinks the editor contacted you.
- There was a glitch in cyberspace and the editor's email never made it to your inbox.
- The editor is a jerk and is trying to use your columns for free.

While it's easy to jump right to the last conclusion, it's more likely that one of the first four explanations fits your scenario. Really. When papers print my column without informing me, I give them the benefit of the doubt. They are busy. They are harried. They meant to email me. They forgot.

In fact, as I was writing this, I decided to Google myself. I found three *(3!)* newspapers that were using my columns – posting them online, even – without ever contacting me. I also found a book group in Fredrickson, Texas that used one of my articles as its discussion piece for the month, but that's fodder for a different book. So, I went ahead and set up a Google Alert on my name. I hadn't before, because it was kind of fun to complete the whole Google process the old-fashioned way. But, it was getting time-consuming. So far, I've found the Google Alert to be a quick and easy way to get the job done.

Note on Google Alert: You key in very specific words that alert your google (so to speak). I've found this isn't a perfect system. The words you key in have to match words posted by the newspaper. I Googled what I thought was obvious: My name, Jill Pertler. With this, I am missing some newspapers that are putting the column online. I know this because they are some of my faithful newspapers – ones that publish me weekly. I could do a second alert, using the name of my column to increase my hits. Even so it's probably a good idea to go in and change up your wording and do your own search every so often. 'Tis not a perfect world.

Note on Google Alert:

You key in very specific words that alert your google (so to speak). I've found this isn't a perfect system.

The good news, as I see it, is that newspapers that are publishing your column without telling you are still publishing your column. Isn't that what you want? In some ways, this can give you the upper hand. They already like your work and are using it. Now what?

When I find a newspaper that is using my column without permission, I send a short, friendly email asking them if this is, in fact, true. Then, I thank them for finding space for the column, and offer to send a photo. That's it. I don't mention payment in this first email. I want to make sure they are really interested in my column first.

When they reply, it is almost always, without question, with an apology. They are sorry they hadn't contacted me. They meant to do so. They like my columns and have been using them weekly, etc.

I reply back, with my headshot (photo) and a request for payment. I outline my basic fees and ask if they have money in their budget for columnists. Each time I've done this, I've got an honest, upfront answer and have been able to form a positive working relationship with the editor.

If you don't get a reply to your initial email (I always have), I would recommend trying again in a couple of days. Double check the newspaper's email address by going to its website. (Although it seems obvious that you are sending to the correct email since they are receiving your columns.) Still, I would check. If the editor fails to respond, you have a choice: keep sending the columns, or stop. Like the whole money thing, this is a personal decision, based on your individual goals and circumstance. Me? I don't know if I want to work with an editor that refuses to communicate with me. So far – thankfully – this hasn't happened.

SAMPLE

Invoice

date

client/newspaper	
email/contact information	
contact person	

Project description

Column name and dates published

Amount billed

Amount due

Thank you for your business!

Your name here.
Name of your column here.

Email address
Phone number

Please send payment to:
Your address.

Legal statement about interest can go here.
Something like:
Net due 30 days from invoice date. Interest of 1.5 percent monthly (18% APR) will accrue on unpaid balances after 30 days.

How it's all organized. Keeping track of your self-syndication progress is no small task. It requires lots of files and folders. Mine starts with one large ***Syndication*** folder and branches out from there. Here's how I have my information organized on my computer. The folders are in bold type.

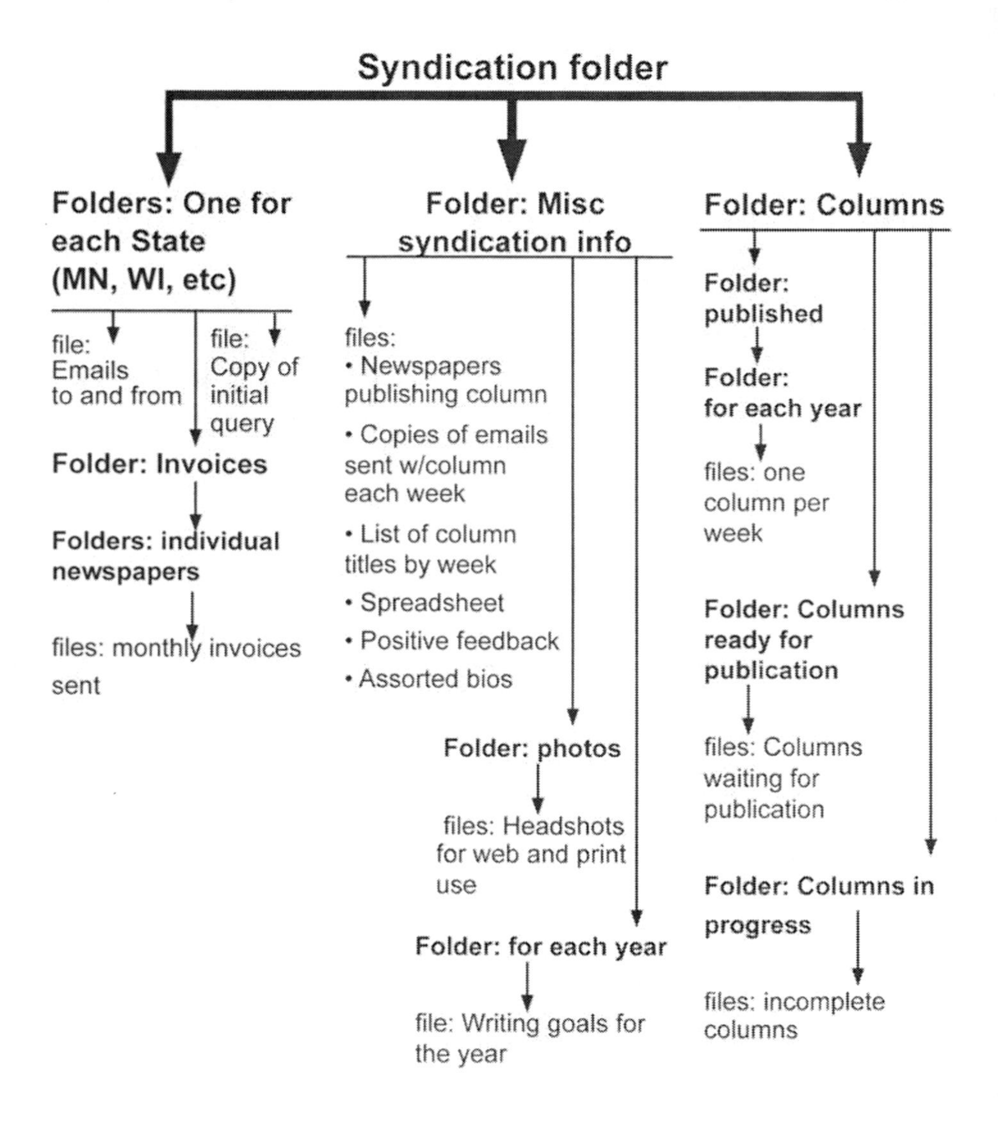

11.

Chapter 11

Time management: *Where you can expect yours to go*

Writers like to write. Columnists are writers. You should spend the bulk of your time putting the pen to the paper (or at least typing at your computer), right (or is that write)?

In an ideal world, this would be the case. But, as a self-syndicated columnist, you are a business owner, bookkeeper, photographer, administrative assistant, webmaster, sales person, secretary, director of marketing, office manager, bill collector, software procurement specialist, editor, grammar checker, spelling whiz, IT manager and CEO of columns – all at the same time. It is a necessity that you spend time doing things other than writing. The success of your business depends on it.

Finding a balance that works for you is key. Just like you can't afford to spend all your time writing, you can't let complex spreadsheets or the task of keeping your address book up-to-date waylay your schedule. You have to find a time for everything by giving everything its time. (Easier said than done.)

We all know that writing can get pushed to the backburner. There are so many other things that fill your day – kids, pets, husbands, laundry, dirty toilets – real glamorous stuff. Glamour or not, the regular stuff has to get done. You may work at a regular and respectable day job, and have to squeeze writing in on the side. How is that possible?

It can be done. But, you are going to have to make writing a priority. Yes – you have to put writing right up there with dental appointments and giving the dog a bath. You make writing your priority (one of them anyway) by scheduling it into your day (or week, or month). If you have a calendar or PDA, you create a category for "writing." (This blocked out time is not for contacting newspapers, working on your spreadsheet or any other administrative tasks – writing only.) If you set aside just 45 minutes each evening Monday through Friday, you'll have spent nearly four hours writing by the end of the week. Use your lunch hour to write and you have added two-and-a-half hours. It adds up. If you make writing a priority, you can find the time, even if it is a snippet here and a moment there.

I'm not going to beat around the bush. I'm lucky. I write "full-time" (at least it feels full-time to me). I don't have to work around a day job – just

Finding a balance that works for you is key. Just like you can't afford to spend all your time writing, you can't let complex spreadsheets waylay your schedule. You have to find a time for everything by giving everything its time.

four kids, assorted pets and way, way too many dust bunnies.

I spend about 10 hours per week on my column – writing, editing and administrative tasks. But I think this is a very individual thing. You may need lots more or lots less time. I've gotten better (a.k.a. faster) with experience. It used to take me twice as long to write and edit.

In addition to column "stuff," I spend another 20 hours per week on other writing tasks garnered through my marketing business. For me, 30 hours feels like full-time. I have four kids, a busy family and a husband who enjoys my company every once in awhile. You may have more time. You may have less. The key for me – and just about everyone – is balance.

A "typical" day

On a typical day, I am at my computer by about 9 a.m. (After getting the kids off to school, cleaning up breakfast mess, making sure beds are made and maybe throwing in a load of laundry, cleaning a bathroom, mopping the floor or completing some sort of house-needed task.)

Mondays are my most structured day, because that's when I send out my columns.

Monday mornings, I email my column to newspapers – by 9 a.m. on good days, by noon for sure. I always spend at least 30 minutes (sometimes longer) proofing, reading out loud and doing final edits to the column on Monday morning.

Monday afternoons I deal with email errors and correspondence with papers. It can be a five-minutes-here, five-minutes-there type of task, but I like to stay at my computer so I am able to take care of replies in a quick and timely fashion.

In between reading emails and sending replies, I work on other writing projects. I have a marketing business, so I may be doing a newsletter, brochure, annual report – you get the picture. I don't usually write any *Slices of Life* columns on Monday afternoons.

Monday evenings, I try to get onto Facebook and post my column from the week before. I put it into the Notes section there. This allows newspapers a first-run of the column, but also gives my friends in other states the chance to see my work.

Tuesday, Wednesday and Thursday are miscellaneous workdays. I work on whatever is on the front burner. If I'm between projects, I may compile more email addresses. I would like to process the addresses for one state each week, but that doesn't happen. The good news is that this means I am doing other writing work. The bad news is that it makes the syndication process even more gradual.

By Thursday I may actively try to think of column ideas and get some words down on paper. Just knowing my topic gives me a sense of relief for the week. Often I work on two or three topics at the same time. I finish them, and have a stockpile of columns – just in case. I always try to have one or two completed in advance, but it doesn't always work this way. Friday is a light workday. I may work some on a column, but often not.

I often write columns on the weekends. Maybe it's something about the looming Monday deadline that gives me inspiration. But I typically grab 15 minutes here, 20 minutes there to tap out a few ideas on the computer. They come together on Saturday or Sunday so that I have a column complete with hook of a beginning, artistically meaty middle and a snappy, I-didn't-see-that-one-coming ending.

I spend a few hours each week on administrative stuff. This includes:

Administrative "stuff"

- Managing existing addresses in my address book. There are always a few – and as many as a dozen – each week that come back with errors or some other issue requiring investigation.

- Email correspondence with editors and readers. On Mondays, I get at least a handful of emails. Other days maybe one or two. I always try to respond back within 24 hours.

- Invoicing. I do this once each month. I have one master invoice set up and then just fill in the blanks. I spend about five minutes per invoice. This includes the invoice and updating information on my spreadsheet.

- Keeping track of newspapers published and circulation numbers. I try to keep on top of these numbers by recording this information as soon as I get it. I've found if I don't, I forget!

- Website updates. Some weeks this doesn't take any time, others it can take a couple of hours. I ask newspapers to contact me if they run my column on their website. When they do, I provide a link on my website.

- Social networking – Facebook, Twitter, writing websites etc. As you social networkers out there know, this can take a little – or a lot – of your time. Some weeks, I am so busy with other things that I hardly have a moment to venture from my work. Other weeks, I can spend 30 minutes (or more) each day networking within the various online sites – that adds up.

- Backing up files. This means columns, spreadsheets, your address book and everything in between. I put them on a portable hard drive.

- Printing a hard copy of my column and filing it in a three-ring binder. I'm old-fashioned, I guess. Still want a hard copy.

- Investigating Google Alerts or do a Google search to see where my column is appearing online.

- Going to the bank to cash paychecks. I try to keep this to once a week. Grin. But it would be fun to have to go everyday, wouldn't it?

Where the time goes

Writing the initial column takes anywhere from one to three hours, and then another one to two hours of editing. I like to write a little and then take a break. Return to the computer, write and edit some more, etc. I call it snippet-writing; it's the process that seems to work for me. (It probably developed as a result of me having four young children when I started this gig. They never let me stay at the computer for too long.)

If I am adding email addresses from a new state to my collection, that can take anywhere from two to 10 hours in a week. It is a time-consuming project. This only happens when I don't have any other writing or editing projects on my desk.

When you add up the hours, it doesn't seem like a lot: a few hours for administration, a few for writing and a few more for editing. We might be talking 10 hours per week. If 100 papers pay you just $5 per week, that's $500, or $50 per hour, for all your time spent – writing, editing and administration. Not bad.

12.

Chapter 12

Other opportunities for exposure and promoting your column

The Internet has changed the world, but you already knew that. It has changed the way we get information as well as the way we send and disseminate information. It provides opportunities to spread the good news about our syndicated column. Most of the information and writing advice on the World Wide Web tells us to establish an online presence. We want to develop name recognition and branding of our product. We are told to get out there, get our words out there and make our column be known!

This can be a good thing… or not. There are pros and cons regarding splashing your syndicated columns all over the Internet. I think of it as a large buffet dinner. There's lots of food there, but not all of it is good for my diet. If I fill my plate with everything, that very well may be too much. When it comes to an online presence, I prefer an everything-inmoderation approach. Many writers look at any online exposure as good exposure. I don't see it that way. I look at exposure opportunities from a standpoint of whether they will help me advance toward my long-term writing goals. For me, this means increased circulation and getting my column published in more newspapers. To achieve that goal, I want to keep newspapers happy. Keeping newspapers happy does not always mean a bigger online presence. This more-is-not-necessarily-better viewpoint makes me different from about 95 percent of writers working the Internet scene.

My message? Don't post your column without thinking about how and why a particular posting will benefit you. Many times it will be beneficial to share your column at different places online. Just be sure you know what you are doing when you do.

Commonly listed advantages of a blog

- Blogging is like writing practice; it makes you better and faster.

- A blog helps build your writing experience. If your writing resume is sparse, a blog is one way to fill in some of the blanks.

- A blog helps you establish credibility as an expert regarding a certain topic. It helps you establish your online presence and brand identity.

- Readers of your blog give you feedback, making you a better writer.

- Putting your words out there – online – for the entire world to see builds confidence.

- A blog keeps you in touch with your readers. It's sort of like a phone call home to mom.

Blogging, why you (maybe) should and why I don't

Blogs are used to give commentary, provide information, establish a personal or business identity and sell ideas and products. Individuals, groups or businesses all use blogs for different purposes. They are a successful force in numerous situations. If you do a little online research, you'll find lots of information advising writers to have and maintain a blog.

Writers are advised to blog because it gives them writing experience and practice; feedback from readers can make them a better and faster writer. A blog adds substance to an empty resume. Blogging builds a writer's confidence. These may seem like good reasons to get out there and start a blog ASAP. It may well be that a blog is right for you, depending on your specific needs and goals.

Besides, many writers have blogs. They use these to gain readership and a following. A blog almost seems like a requirement these days.

> *Q: Where's your blog?*
> *A: What blog?*
> *Q: Don't you want to use it to establish your online presence?*
> *A: I'm not sure.*

A personal blog is pretty easy to acquire. You set it up and type... type... type away. You don't need an editor's approval to have a blog. There are no deadlines. No word counts. No one pays you a fee for reading or printing your blog. In fact, you can't even call your words a column or article. They are called blog entries.

But what about all those touted benefits? Take a look at them again: A blog is like writing practice. Feedback from readers can make you a better writer. Blogging builds credibility, confidence and your resume. It keeps you in touch. These are benefits, to be sure. But, are they benefits that pertain to you? If you are looking at self-syndication, you have an established column. You have your voice. You have practiced writing – by writing your column – for readers and editors in the real world. Will a blog create more opportunities for you to get your columns published in newspapers? Will it make it more likely that newspapers will pay you?

How will a blog benefit you?

A little background:

According to Wikipedia, as of December 2007, one search engine – Technorati – was racking more than 112 million blogs. Wow. Wiki then goes on to say that many people take pride in their blog posts – even if they are never read. Never read? Why would I write something just so it could be never read? I might be missing the obvious, but that doesn't seem like a good way to gain name recognition.

Be honest here: how many blogs do you read each day? How much time do you set aside for blog reading each week? Each month? How many blogs do you have bookmarked because they are just that good? I thought so.

A blog is a passive way to put your words on the Internet. You blog and wait... wait... for people to come to your site to read your thoughts. I don't know the ins and outs of gaining advertising dollars through a blog, but gaining advertisers seems like time spent selling versus writing. Blogging just doesn't seem like a sure-fire winning way to utilize my time as a writer and meet my long-term writing goals. (As a business owner looking to sell widgets... well, that may be another story.)

Besides, for me, a blog too closely mirrors what I write in my columns. I write about my everyday life; a personal blog is like a diary. If I blog about something online – for free – and then I turn the blog into an article, it seems like newspapers will be less likely to print it, much less pay me for my work.

I look at my weekly column as a blog of sorts: Each week, I get more practice writing my column. Feedback from readers (and publishers and editors) makes me a better writer. Having a weekly syndicated column builds my credibility, confidence and resume. It keeps me in touch with my readers. Sound like the same benefits a blog is purported to deliver? I thought so.

People who follow my column are some of the same who would follow a blog. By being in 70 newspapers and 150,000 households each week, I daresay I am reaching more people than I would with a very successful blog.

So, at the risk of being hunted down and flogged by bloggers, I don't maintain a blog to promote my column.

There I said it. I've never been one to follow the crowd. I have my reasons, and I've tried to be thoughtful about my decision. There are only so many hours in the day (24 at last count) and I don't think using mine to blog to promote my syndicated column would be time well spent. Using a blog to promote a book, however, might be a different story entirely. As would using a blog to promote your business or other venture. *I am only talking about non-blogging as it relates to a syndicated column.*

I may change my stance on this at some point (I am always re-thinking and re-planning). But for now I feel comfortable with an unblogging, non-blog, sans-blog status.

I look at my weekly column as a blog of sorts. The people who follow my column are some of the same who would follow a blog.

Website presence and posting

I have a website. I do think it is one Internet necessity – if nothing else, it provides credibility. But, what do you include on your website? Do you post your columns weekly? I don't.

I probably could, if I delayed publication to a week after they are disbursed to newspapers. But my main focus is getting my column published in newspapers (either in their paper copy, online or both). So if I am serving as my own online newspaper, by posting my columns at my website, I am sort of kicking my own goals in the butt. My line of thinking is this: why should a newspaper pay me for my words if the same material is available for everyone to see – for free – online? Many newspapers post their current issue online for everyone to view. Then, after a week or so, they charge a fee to access archived articles. I think one smart technique is to use my website to direct readers to the newspaper sites that carry my columns. It's just one more way to promote my column while keeping newspapers happy at the same time.

I see less of a problem with posting columns a week or two after they appear in print editions. That way, you are only impacting a newspaper's re-sell fee for your columns. I'm guessing this isn't significant – not that your column isn't supercalifragilistic. My logic tells me that not many people purchase old articles or columns from newspapers online.

Many writers look at any online

exposure as good exposure.

I don't see it that way.

So, I don't post fresh columns on my website; I only post those that have had their newspaper run. That's okay. I have plenty of other materials to put on the web. You can include your bio information – in more detail than the two-sentence blurb used with your column. You can give a history of your column. You can showcase other writing projects that you've done. You can advertise your writing business. You can provide links to other useful sites.

What I do (or should) post on my website:

- Positive feedback received from readers and editors.
- Good news of my syndication numbers: "*Slices of Life* is now published in 70 newspapers!
- A complete listing of the newspapers that carry the column, with links to those that post the column online.
- An invitation for readers to contact their editor if they'd like to see it in their own local paper.
- Speaking engagements with locations and dates.
- Links to news or other website postings about my column or writing.
- Links to Twitter, Facebook and useful writing sites that I frequent.
- Awards or other accolades I happen to garner.
- A link to purchase this book.
- Other writing work I've done.

A website is a useful tool. It can provide your readers with lots of information and it can help to increase name recognition, establish your platform and brand. It can gain you a fan base. Just make sure you are not usurping the role of the newspapers by asking them to pay you for information that you've posted on your website for all to see – for free.

Facebook, Twitter and other social networking sites

There are lots of places to do social networking online. You could spend 24 hours a day just getting social with your network. Because of the plethora of options out there, you have to make some choices. You can't possibly network (and do a quality job of it) at every social site available.

When investigating various social networking options, ask yourself the age-old question: What is in it for me? Can the site help you gain readers? Colleagues? Will it be an easy way for you to promote your column? Will it further your writing career in some way? How much time does each particular site require? Can you make that time commitment?

Different networking sites will serve different purposes for your writing life. Some will promote your work. Others may provide you with writing information and support. For my purposes, I participate in Facebook, Twitter and a few online writing forums.

Facebook

Facebook is a force that can't (and shouldn't) be ignored; it is the number one social networking site in the world. According to Facebook's press room, it has more than 400 million active users (note word *active*), with half of those users logging on to Facebook on any given day. Demographics show that Facebook isn't just for teenagers anymore. Information for 2009 (according to iStrategyLabs) shows the largest growth in users – a whopping 276 percent – occurred with individuals who were 35 to 54 years old. What started as a social and recreational outlet for college students has grown into a professional business opportunity for adults, and provides an outlet for columnists, like me, to make my work (and words) grow. One caveat: the average user spends nearly an hour (55 minutes) on Facebook each day; beware that it doesn't become a drain on your time.

Facebook gives you three account options for setting up information within its site: you can set up a personal profile, a group or a Facebook page.

Personal profiles are best for the obvious – personal use. They are the basis for Facebook: friends communicating with friends. Information exchanged is personal in nature – observations on what you had for lunch, what's on TV or the results of your son's soccer game. Personal profiles require a reciprocal relationship. That is, you have to request access to someone's profile, and they have to confirm that access. This is called being someone's "friend." When you are friends with someone on Facebook, you have access to their personal profile information and vice versa.

Groups are meant for organizing, but on a personal level – for smaller scale interaction around a cause and to foster group discussion around a certain topic or hobby, like knitting or memoir writing. Anyone can set up and join a group. You can be a member of the knitting group without being a Facebook friend with everyone in the group.

Pages are intended to help a person or company communicate publicly. Facebook gives you two options when creating pages: the official page (also called fan page) and community page. A community page is set up to generate support for a cause or topic; for instance, to garner backing for a political candidate or to encourage a cause such as recycling. A fan page is created to help brands, businesses, bands, movies, celebrities and syndicated columnists communicate and provide information to followers, or fans. Like a group, a Facebook page allows you to interact with others without being connected to their personal profile account. Your fans can see your fan page, but you can't see their personal profiles. In order to set up a fan page, you have to be an official representative of the entity that's collecting fans, i.e. your column.

Originally I promoted my syndicated column through a personal profile page. (As a rookie, I didn't realize there were other Facebook options.) I used Facebook's notes feature to post my columns a week after they were printed in newspapers. I did this so that my friends living outside my column's circulation area could have access to my words. It was a way to build a following and readership – on a small scale. When you post a Facebook note, you have the option of who can see it: your friends, friends of friends or everyone. This gives you control of how far and wide your words are distributed. I posted the columns a week after they were printed so that newspapers had the chance to publish the column first. I didn't want to put myself in competition with the newspapers in any way.

While the personal profile worked okay for promoting my column, I think a fan page is a better choice. A page allows you access to information that profiles and groups don't. This includes number of new fans, number of visits to your page and fan demographics. Facebook even sends you an email with a weekly summary of activity for your page. It's useful information for someone trying to grow a syndicated column. In addition, you don't gum up your column (professional) information with your profile (personal) info. Fans don't necessarily want to know that your cat threw up on the couch again or that your latte tastes great this morning.

When creating a page, you will be asked to categorize your organization. Under the "Artist, band or public figure" tab is the option of "writer." Bingo – that's you! Type in your page name (i.e. name of your column), certify that you are an official representative of your column (with a click of your mouse) and you are good to go. Facebook page created.

While waiting for all your fans to flock to your page, you can add content and make it interesting so that those fans will want to visit often and much. This starts with posting your column as a note (after it's appeared in newspapers), but that is only the beginning. Insightful remarks, quotes and useful links all fit within the category of making things more interesting.

It goes without saying (but I will anyway) that your photo (headshot) should be uploaded onto your Facebook page. You want to do everything you can to tie the page in with your column.

I use my name, photo, copies of the column, the name of the column and a tagline to further hone in on my message. A tagline is a short, one or two sentence ditty that sums up the meaning and idea of your column.

The tagline I use for *Slices of Life* is: *One should never be too full for dessert. You don't have to eat the whole pie, but you probably have room for a small slice.* This sort of says it all. You don't have time to read a whole book, but you should take a little time out for some fun. Come and be entertained by a small slice of a column that is so pleasurable it feels like a good dessert.

Finally, Facebook is a way to collect positive feedback from fans. Each week, when I post my column, I get positive comments from various friends and fans. When posted on Facebook, these positive comments promote my work and encourage others to take a few minutes to read the column for the week (and perhaps even contact the editor of their local newspaper to suggest publishing my column).

But that isn't all. I cut and paste each positive comment into my testimonial file (along with emails from editors and readers). They can be used now – or later – on my website, Twitter and other promotional materials. The more positive comments I can amass, the better.

While I am on Facebook, promoting my work and hoping to collect fans, I can do so by being a fan as well. Look for newspapers that are on Facebook (there are lots out there). Become a friend or fan (depending on the type of account they have set up) and foster a relationship that way. If you are a fan of a newspaper, it is more likely they will visit your page and become a fan of yours.

Twitter

Setting up a Twitter account is very easy. I suggest using a name that ties in with you and/or your column. I went with plain old "JillPertler." Upload your column headshot onto Twitter and you are good to go.

This venue isn't large enough for an entire column. Obviously. But, you can use Twitter in much the same way you use Facebook – except in shorter bursts. You can direct people to newspaper websites that carry your column. Post a couple (or more) each day if you're prone to tweeting. This would increase the hits your column gets online and is a benefit to the newspapers carrying your column.

If you receive an especially eloquent tidbit of praise from an editor or reader, you might want to share the quote with your Twitter-base. Quotes on the art and craft of writing are always welcome, as are links to well-written articles on various writing topics.

I am a newbie tweeter, still looking for new ways to spread my wings within this forum. Twitter may limit your keystrokes, but there's no limit to your imagination and what you can do with those strokes. So twitter away. Anything that you can use to benefit yourself, your column and newspapers sounds like a good idea to me. Just remember the key word: benefit. Don't post unless it pads your nest. Peep. Peep.

Forums and chat groups

I belong to a few writing sites. I find them very supportive and useful sources of information. They are also a great way to share good news about your column, where it is published and how people can access (i.e. read) it.

I am not overly chatteristic. I tend to watch and read posts rather than making them myself – most of the time. (Like a lot of writers, I'm more of a behind-the-scenes person than an in-your-face one.) But the folks I have met through writing forums have been great. When I have posted an idea or question I have always received good sound advice and

Because of the nature of our business, many writers are pretty isolated. Most days I know it's just me and the corner of my living room.

information. For instance, when I posted in reply to a question about writing a syndicated column, I got two offers to write articles on the topic, which morphed into the idea that generated this book.

In general, forums are used for information exchange and question and answer-type stuff. They are a way to share information, but not a place for overzealous self-promotion. You can tell members "good news" of your writing successes. You can include syndication information (your web address, name of your column, etc.) in your forum signature. You can answer questions (from other forum members) regarding your areas of expertise. But, unless you are purchasing an advertisement from a particular forum or website, this isn't the place to splash a large and flashy self-promotion about your new syndicated column. There may be a venue for this within the forum, but you want to check with the forum supervisor before posting anything that is questionable. For me, it seems like common sense. But, it is easy to get carried away with momentum of your writing and promotion of that writing. You don't want to harm future relationships by posting without thinking – or checking with the forum administrator – first. If in doubt, ask.

Forums can also be a source for other writing opportunities. You may write a column, but chances are you write other things as well. I've gotten freelance assignments and entered writing contests all because of information found on various writing forums and websites. It's all there for the taking, and in many cases, it's free.

Because of the nature of our business, many writers are pretty isolated. Most days, I know it's just me and the corner of my living room. There isn't anyone to run ideas by or approach with questions. It cuts down on time spent on office gossip, but it can also get a little lonely. If nothing else, forums and online discussion groups encourage me to write more and better. That's sort of a roundabout way of promoting my column, but I'll take it.

Email signature

Remember the ideas of gaining name recognition while connecting your moniker with the title of your column? Your email signature is a great place to do this. Every time you send an email (and if you are like me you do this many times each day) you are reminding editors, publishers and readers of your name, the name of your column and the fact that these two things are intertwined.

Set up an email signature to use with all your syndication correspondence in the Preferences section of your email program. For me, this requires clicking on Mail, then Preferences and finally Signature. For your self-syndication signature, you'll want to include: Your name, the name of your column and the fact that it is syndicated and a link to your website.

Other information that you might want to consider including: phone numbers, a tagline, a link to your blog, an invitation to your Facebook page, your Twitter address and a link to a newspaper that posts your column each week.

When creating your signature, you might be tempted to get creative with font choices and colors. The more the better, right? Not usually. Choose an easy-to-read font – Arial, Helvetica or Times if you like serifs (the little endcap lines on letters). If you get too funky, your font may not make it through cyberspace. Most email programs readily accept certain fonts. Stick with the basics and you'll do fine.

Once you pick your font, stay with it. It's okay to vary the size of your font from line to line, but again, don't go overboard. The same goes for italics (oblique) and bold. A little goes a long way. As far as colors go, it's okay to use a couple, but beyond that, you'll lose your reader to your rainbow. I use a dark gray and deep crimson in my signature. Both colors are easy to read and not too shocking to the eye.

My address book software allows me to upload a photo as part of my address header. This is a perfect spot for the headshot that accompanies my column. The mantra: branding and name recognition.

FOR INSTANCE

My email signature looks like this, with a few select words in crimson:

Jill Pertler *(crimson)*
Marketing by Design
Writing and design services *(crimson)*

author of the syndicated column:
Slices of Life *(crimson)*
"One should never be too full for dessert. You don't have to eat the whole pie, but you probably have room for a small slice."

pertmn@qwest.net

phone number(s) could go here

website:
http://marketing-by-design.home.mchsi.com

Read ***Slices*** each week at:
http://www.pinejournal.com/

Visit me on Facebook: address here.
Tweet me on Twitter: Information here.

Public speaking (eek!)

I am a writer not a public speaker! The thought of standing in front of a crowd – all eyes on me – having to communicate my thoughts (out loud) is not my idea of a dream day. But, like invoicing, publicly and verbally spreading news of your column and other writing efforts is an important and worthwhile part of the job.

I'm not a huge public speaker (surprise, surprise). But, I have found that I can do it. This is leaps and bounds ahead of where I was with this a year ago.

If you are asked to speak to a group, consider it a great compliment. They see you as an expert. That's pretty cool.

After accepting the invitation, consider the group and what sort of information might interest them. How many will be in the group? You can talk with the person who extended the speaking invitation about these details. You want to be ready to speak and answer questions about the topics that are of specific interest to the group.

Before the big day, take some time to prepare. Jot notes. Make an outline. Even if the session is planned to be question and answer, you will want to have some information prepared for those quiet, in-between-question moments.

Reflect on your writing experiences and come up with a few interesting anecdotes that you can share with the group. What were some of your best learning moments? Did you ever mess up terribly and then go on to

If you are asked to speak to a group, consider it a great compliment. They see you as an expert. That's pretty cool.

correct your mistake? What made you decide to become a writer? How does your writing process work?

If you think you may be asked to read your work, have something ready. Review some of your pieces and pick the one that you think would be an appropriate fit with your audience. Then, practice reading it out loud.

Put together a short bio on yourself – a paragraph or so in length. Don't be overly modest. If you have won writing awards or have significant experience, include it. You can use this to introduce yourself, or (better yet) to have someone introduce you.

Practice in front of a mirror or with a friend or family member. Have them ask you questions, if possible. Don't memorize answers. You want to be natural and conversational – and prepared.

Assemble your presentation materials before the day of your appearance. Remember: business cards, an outline of potential speaking topics and personal anecdotes, a couple selections of items that you might read and your bio.

If you are unfamiliar with the location where you'll be speaking, visit it ahead of time. Will you be in front of an audience, or sitting together – perhaps in a circle – for a group discussion?

Arrive early. Do not jog in, huffing and puffing, five minutes late. If you are nervous about speaking, this will only serve to make you feel on the spot and ill-prepared. (Not to mention making you look on-the-spot, ill-prepared and unprofessional.) Come early. Get your bearings. Review your notes. Breathe.

Realize that some amount of nervousness is a positive thing. Even the pros get nervous. In small amounts it provides a sort of magic energy that can add to your presentation.

Admit your shortcomings. One of my Eureka moments came when I was talking to a group of high school students and I fielded a question about public speaking. When I confessed that I found it challenging – and especially challenging to address a group of high schoolers – it felt like a weight had been lifted off my chest. It's okay to say, "I'm a writer. Not a public speaker, but I will do my best to speak publicly with you today." It makes you refreshingly human, I think.

Write a book

A book can be used to promote your column, and vice versa. I also think that being a published author gives you a certain amount of credibility – with newspaper editors and publishers. It helps to establish you as an expert in your field.

I've often wondered, which comes first, the column or the book? Perhaps it doesn't matter. Some book authors become columnists because of the subject matter of their book. Others, like me, are columnists first, with the book growing as an offshoot of the column.

Either way, I think a book benefits a column and a column benefits a book. It is a mutual reciprocity, symbiotic sort of working arrangement. That's always a good thing.

Which comes first, the column or the book?

Perhaps it doesn't matter.

13.

Chapter 13

Miscellaneous: Copyright, vacations, fans and more

Copyrights

What does that little © mean?

According to the U.S. government, copyright is protection provided by law (title 17, U.S. Code) to "original works of authorship," as soon as they are recorded in tangible form.

Copyright protection is frequently misunderstood. Every creative work is copyrighted the moment it is fixed in tangible form. No publication or registration or other action in the Copyright Office is required to secure copyright. No notice (i.e. displaying that little © symbol) is necessary, though it helps legal cases. No registration is necessary, though it could make things easier when you sue the fool who stole your words. A copyright lasts until 70 years after the author dies. Facts and ideas can't be copyrighted, only expressions of creative effort.

To summarize: If you do nothing, your articles will still legally be copyrighted. This stays in place until 70 years after your death.

This is true whether you use the copyright symbol or not. I don't use one, but after writing this section, I might start. Why not? It acts as a reminder. It lets people who aren't versed in copyright law know that your article is protected. It discourages anyone from stealing your work. For extra effect, add your name and the year next to the copyright symbol.

To ensure legal proof that your work is, indeed, your own, you can file for a formal copyright with the U.S. Copyright Office. Your copyright will be put on public record. You can do all this online. Current fees are $35 for a basic claim (when completed online) the fee increases to $50 if you use a fill-in form and mail it via the postal service.

For more information, check out the U.S. Copyright Office at www.copyright.gov.

Do columnists get vacations?

Excuse me for a moment. I need to step up on my soapbox. Everyone needs a vacation. Everyone benefits from a vacation. I highly recommend vacations. They keep you sane. They help you relax. They promote creative thought. The experiences you have while on a vacation can give you some great material for your writing.

Do columnists get vacations? That is a facetious question. As a columnist – a self-syndicated columnist – you are your own boss. You are in charge of office policy. Give yourself a vacation!

I wrote 52 columns during my first year after going weekly. Even though I produced the equivalent of a column each week, I managed to take time off. I did this by writing ahead and sending two columns out the week before a planned vacation.

I also advocate for having a few completed columns in the hopper in case of family emergency, illness or accident. This is your insurance policy. Sometimes I find myself operating without insurance, however. Such is the life of a reckless and renegade writer.

Now that I have an established working relationship with numerous newspapers, I officially take two weeks off each year: Christmas week and the week of July Fourth. During these weeks, I send an "evergreen, classic column." In other words, it's a favorite that's been run before – usually three or more years before, so it feels new to most eyes. I let newspapers know well in advance (about a month) of my impending vacation. That way if they don't like the idea of re-running a classic column, they have ample time to formulate a plan B for that week.

With the onslaught of wireless Internet, it is completely possible to have a working vacation. I have done that in the past, but my biggest obstacle has been my address book. I've run into various snags when trying to copy my addresses from my hard drive onto a flash and then onto my laptop. My addresses are organized in folders and those folders lose their integrity when making the move from computer to computer. It can be done, however. I would just make sure that I had everything intact and ready to go – on my laptop – before ever packing a suitcase.

Dealing with fans... or, readers

I've found there are three types of people who respond favorably to my column: readers, fans and people who want something. Readers are the best. They email because they are touched by my work. Nothing more. Nothing less.

If there's anything better than having your writing recognized favorably by editors and publishers, it's having the same thing happen with readers. Readers will email. They will stop you on the street. I'm not gonna lie. It's sort of fun.

When a reader emails regarding a certain column, I am moved. For someone to read my words and be touched to the extent that they will email is overwhelming and kind. I typically send a reply email – short and sweet, thanking them for taking the time to contact me.

There have been times when I've received an email that is over-the-top in its praises. In this case, the note came from what I call a fan. Fans are good; they just see me as greater than human. I am the best writer in the world. From what I have written, my fan knows that I am the best wife and mother. I am the best, most beautiful person ever born. This type of email is overwhelming in a different way; it's too good to be true. Again, I send a short and sweet thank-you email. Then, before hitting the send button, I delete my phone numbers from the signature portion of my email. No sense taking chances.

Every once in awhile, I receive an email from someone who read my column, likes my work and thinks I would be a perfect fit to help him or her with a certain project. I've been approached to help with college essays, entrepreneurial ventures and even marriage counseling. The requests all have one thing in common; they are random and have little or no logical connection with my actual column. For whatever reason, this person feels I can help them with (fill in the blank here). Is the request an innocent one, or is it laced with ulterior motives? I'm never sure. I try to give the person the benefit of the doubt. I answer their email, providing brief, helpful information (if I can and if the situation warrants it). I kindly decline their offer and again, I delete my phone numbers from the signature line of my email.

When a reader emails regarding a certain column, I am moved. For someone to read my words and be touched to the extent that they will email is overwhelming and kind.

Hate mail

Occasionally, I hear from a fourth type of reader: one who hates my column.

Over the course of three years, I have received a couple negative emails. One person called my article alarming and obnoxious and accused me of being a miserable and selfish person; she came to this conclusion after reading the first three paragraphs of one of my columns. She didn't even finish the article! Another reader wrote to say that I had obviously never stood at the bus stop with a child on dark winter morning. This was in response to a tongue-in-cheek article suggesting that we do away with daylight savings time. I tell ya, some people take life too seriously.

My reason for telling you about these instances is twofold. First, I have received hundreds comments about my articles and columns; many have been positive; two have been negative. Guess which two I can remember in detail?

I think as humans we are wired that way – to remember the negative and forget the positive. I don't know how to change that about myself. Hopefully sharing it with you will help you to better deal with a negative comment should one ever come your way.

Second, when I receive a critical email, my first instinct is to fire back a nasty note that hits below the belt and knocks 'em out cold. I could do it, too. I am a woman of words, after all. It's tempting to think that it would feel satisfying to lash back at anger with anger. But it wouldn't do any good. And, it would only feel satisfying for about 30 seconds. Anger doesn't get you anywhere – at least not anywhere that you want to go.

I could ignore the negative note. It's definitely an option. But, then the sender might not know that I received his or her message. They might feel the need to write again. If I ignore the note, I am missing an opportunity to (attempt) to reach out to a reader in a positive way. (Even though this person wrote me a hate note, they still read my column and are technically a reader.)

When I receive a negative comment, I do respond – carefully. I always thank the naysayer for their email. And then, I tell them that the email "made my day." I go on to say that a columnist is looking for an emotionally-charged reaction and their angst only goes to show that my words are touching people and doing exactly what I want them to do. And then I remove my phone numbers from the signature of my email. Anyone who can get irate after reading just three paragraphs of one of my columns does not need access to my phone numbers.

Here's why I do what I do: I approach anger with kindness because the experts tell us that anger, if unfueled, dissipates rather quickly. I have been angry before and haven't enjoyed it one bit. If I can help an angry person to dissipate, I'm all for it. I am also approaching their anger with honesty. As a writer I am looking for (hoping for) emotionally-charged reactions to my work. Reaching readers means tapping into their emotions – in (usually) positive and (occasionally) negative ways. In this particular case, I touched a nerve. Something about my writing got to this person. That isn't all bad.

Whenever I respond to a reader, fan, request or hate mail, I make sure my note is free of errors and typos. I want to represent myself in a positive way, and that means mistakes are a no-no. I also make sure that whatever I write could be copied and distributed and I wouldn't be upset, embarrassed or angry. Whenever you create an email and press send, the recipient has the option of forwarding to everyone in their address book, posting your note on Facebook and/or putting it on their website. Remember that. Always be careful; and be especially careful with readers… or, fans.

Reader email distribution list?

I keep track of feedback from readers. I reply to their emails. But I could take it a step further. I could place them on an email distribution list. I could send my columns weekly. I could send information about speaking engagements or the publication of this book.

At this point, I don't do that. If I ever did, I would get permission from each reader before placing him or her on a distribution list. Why? Because it is the respectful thing to do. In the past, I have emailed various writers, to provide them with positive feedback, to ask questions or to respond to a question that they may have had. Every so often, one of those writers puts me on his or her distribution list and I get generic emails that I never requested. This puts me in a difficult position. I don't want to disrespect the other writer by asking to be taken off their list (we do operate in a professional community after all). On the other hand, the unrequested emails serve as an irritant (and are not exactly professional).

I subscribe to a few email newsletters. The key word here is "subscribe." If you decide to email your column (or other information) out to a distribution list of readers and fans, make sure that they have subscribed to your service – and that you provide them an "unsubscribe" outlet. Readers may readily accept your columns as a guest in their homes, but don't overstay your welcome.

Creative uses for syndication

Sometimes it's not what you say, but how you say it

The clever writer is a multitasker. And a self-syndicated columnist is clever – if nothing else. What other writer gets paid over and over for the same set of 500 words?

I've found there are other, clever, uses for syndication. Here's one. I write for a regional glossy magazine that is owned by a large newspaper conglomerate. One of my regular assignments is writing an article for the inside back page of the magazine. In order to tie the article in with my syndicated column, I call it *The Last Slice.* (Clever, huh?)

For the last four years, I've been freelancing with a contract that gives the large conglomerate first rights to my work – including *The Last Slice.* Three months after publication, the rights return to me and I am free to re-publish my articles elsewhere.

Well, come the first of the year, the lawyers from corporate came up with a new freelance contract that demanded not only first rights, but all rights to a freelancer's work. Forever. And ever. That was too much for me. The article I write for the back page of the magazine is very personal. I was unwilling to give up my personal stories to corporate. I discussed this with the editor of the magazine and she understood my dilemma. So we went to the lawyers. They said a contract is a contract and is clearly much more important than any personal story could ever be. They told me to sign. Or else.

I'm old enough and stubborn enough (and I've been at this writing stuff long enough) to know that I wasn't going to sign away my rights – even if it meant giving up that back page. I am at a point in my career where I don't have to sign away all my rights. I wasn't mad, just decisive. When I told this to my husband, he just shook his head. He does that sometimes.

But, a writer is clever. I wasn't done with this situation yet. I thought about the back page articles and I thought about my columns and I came up with a proposal. I asked the magazine if they would be interested in working with me not as a freelancer, but as a syndicated columnist. I offered them *The Last Slice* as a syndicated column.

Can you guess their response? They asked if there would be an extra charge for working with me as a syndicated columnist. In other words, they said yes! So, technically, I have two syndicated columns. How clever is that?

The state of the newspaper world

There have been some pretty doomsday reports out there. Newspapers are struggling. I see it firsthand when I get a column returned as undeliverable via email and I do a quick search for the newspaper in question. Too often I find an article describing that newspaper's recent bankruptcy. Newspapers are failing; if they fall, what will become of the columnist?

Are we in a dying profession? I don't think so.

Newspapers are all about providing information. The way we receive information is changing. But, our need for information is not. In fact, I think it may be growing. More and more, people want to know about what is happening around the block and around the world. And, whether that information is received through a printed newspaper or computer news feed, someone has to write it.

The need for good writers is not dwindling with the newspaper industry. Far from it!

People look to a newspaper or news feed for information, but they also come to be entertained. I believe that to be true. So, where there will always be a need for good, quality writers, there will also be a need for good, quality writers who can entertain. That's what a columnist does – entertains and informs.

Whether I entertain and inform in printed form or online doesn't matter, as long as people are reading my words and experiencing my message. If the print version of a newspaper becomes extinct, but it goes on to live online, the good, quality writers will continue to survive. In fact we will thrive.

Some of the small newspapers that I send my column to can't run it in their print edition every week because they have space constraints. Paper space is money. It doesn't work that way online. A paper that can't run my column in its print edition often can put it online, because space is unlimited online. There is no paper, no ink – no printing.

Newspapers charge for website ad space, much like they charge for print ads. They can do this while avoiding printing costs. Pretty slick. But it gets even better.

Here's the best part. A print newspaper is sold as a whole. You can't buy just the editorial or sports section. You get the whole paper and you read what interests you. Newspapers track their circulation statistics, but they can't know exactly how many people read each individual article – or column.

Information on how many hits each article gets is available for online newspapers. An editor or publisher can know – with certainty – which columns are being read the most. Ad costs could be based on frequency of hits, as could writer compensation. Good articles and great columns would result in more hits. Good writers and great columnists would be compensated for their talents. Doesn't sound so bad, does it?

So, we mourn the possible passing of print news as we've always known it. Saying goodbye may be sad, but it does not indicate the demise of the columnist. It indicates a change. Not everyone is able to embrace change. In this case, however, I think the change will be one that brings benefits and rewards to talented, quality writers. Count me in!

A final note:

Self-syndication is one of the best things I've done for myself in the last decade. It's improved my writing. It's proved my diligence, dedication and commitment. It's increased my readership, stamina and confidence. At first, I was afraid to open reply emails from newspapers because I feared rejection. Now I know that acceptance and praise outnumber the terse, unfriendly replies. For the most part, everyone wishes me well and appreciates my writing. Currently, over 70 papers in six states publish my column, and that number is growing weekly. (When I wrote my first draft of this book a couple of months ago those numbers were 50 newspapers in five states.)

I am on my way to paying for that college tuition, and who knows... *Maybe there's a book deal in my future.*

14.

Chapter 14

Resources

Sometimes I sit at my computer in the corner of my living room in northern Minnesota during a light snowfall. The house is quiet. Kids are at school. Husband is at work. The dog is sleeping. The cat lies snoozing. The phone stays still. And, while peaceful, it feels a little isolated.

I love being alone with my thoughts. But it's also nice to know that there are resources available when I need them. Thanks to the Internet, resources for writers like me abound!

There are numerous good reasons (besides loneliness) to access other writers and writing websites online. You can find and solicit editing partners.

Q: Will you read my words?
A: Sure, if you'll read mine!

Feedback from other writers can be invaluable in helping you hone your words and message.

I value writing forums and discussion groups not only for the information they provide, but also for the support – both professional and personal. Even though many writers online have never met face-to-face, they have formed friendships that are valued in the writing and real world.

Being a part of "the group" helps to establish your professional legitimacy. You comment on one writing site. You are quoted on another. You ask a question. You answer a question. Your knowledge increases.

Establishing yourself in the hub of the writing buzz gives you information about freelance jobs, contests and other writing opportunities. Being involved with online writing sites is networking in the new millennium.

A note about forums: I've seen writers alienate themselves by making an angry post or clicking the send button before really thinking about their message. When you access a forum, try to be as respectful, positive and kind as possible. Everyone is there to learn and hone their craft. Don't bash people, even if you think their brainpower and writing skills are nonexistent. Be helpful, not hurtful. I've observed the action on enough online forums to know that hurtful doesn't work.

There is a ton of writing information available online. There are numerous writing sites that warrant your consideration. Unless you've conquered time travel, you can't possibly give attention to them all. So much information, so little time. I could probably fill a whole book with places to peruse online, but then you'd never get around to the business of writing your column. It was hard, but I've picked a few favorites here to get you started. I probably missed some very worthy and worthwhile sites. But, I wanted to be brief; so here are some of my favorites:

Favorite online resources and writing sites *(in alphabetical order):*

Absolute Write – *"Write hard. Write true. And write on."* Put together by MacAllister Stone. Classes, resources and forums with lots of active threads on lots of writing topics. Bills itself as the one-stop home for professional and beginning writers. www.absolutewrite.com/

AutoCrit Writing Center – I've just discovered this site, which is put together by Nina Davies, so I'm still exploring. Hundreds of articles on writing. Site is geared toward fiction writing, but hey, writing is writing, right? Piece de resistance: they offer a tool that analyzes your writing, checking for errors and weakness. You can analyze documents of 800 words or less for free (limit of five per day) or you can upgrade to analyze more for a fee. Beware: this analyzing "toy" can be addicting! www.autocrit.com/

Funds For Writers – Put out by C. Hope Clark. Provides three free newsletters (two weekly, one bi-weekly). The bi-weekly newsletter highlights writing opportunities for kids. Cool. Also offers the bi-weekly "Total Funds for Writers" for a $15 annual fee. Clark offers numerous ebooks filled with grants, contests or markets available for purchase at her site, including "Tweetebooks," which are comprised of 20 markets that suit specific writing/genre interests. She also hosts an annual writing contest. www.fundsforwriters.com

Grammar Girl – Quick and dirty tips regarding hot topics such as affect versus effect, dangling participles and ending a sentence with a preposition. This is true wordsmithing fodder only a writer could love. http://grammar.quickanddirtytips.com. (The grammar girl in question is Mignon Fogarty.)

Humor Writer's Org – Through the University of Dayton, Ohio. Free monthly newsletter. Sponsors the Erma Bombeck Writer's Workshop every other year. Writing information. Monthly humor article contest through humorpress.com. www.humorwriters.org/

My Writer's Circle – Chief moderator is Nick Daws. Forum boasting writer to writer critiques, Q and A, writing challenges, games, resources and job threads. www.mywriterscircle.com/

National Society of Newspaper Columnists – Annual contests. Free newsletter. You can elect to be an official member for $50 annually. At: www.columnists.com/

Shaw Guides – Site providing information on "learning vacations," including zillions of writing conferences and workshops. You can look according to topic, date or location. http:// writing.shawguides.com

Steve Slaunwhite – Steve writes about copywriting and offers a free newsletter. I find his information and advice useful and practical. It translates to many types of writing. steveslaunwhite.com/

Writer Advice – B. Lynn Goodwin hosts an annual writing contest. Free quarterly newsletter with lots of (what else) writing advice. Writing resources. Focuses mostly on flash prose and poetry. writeradvice.com/

Writer's Digest – Forum, contests, blogging opportunities and online workshops. The Writer's Digest Annual Competition is a biggie each year. Writer's digest provides a listing of the 101 best writing sites each year. writersdigest.com/

Writers–Editors Network – Founded by Dana K. Cassell. Site linking writers and editors. Hosts an annual writing contest. Lots of free writing information on site. Also offers membership – basic from $29 per year, to premium for $69 per year. www.writers-editors.com

Writers Market – Site that helps you find places to sell your writing, manage submissions and gain current information about the writing industry. Bills itself as the "Freelance writer's bible." Offers a free newsletter. Annual membership is $39.99 or $5.99 per month. www.writersmarket.com/

WritersWeekly.com – Published by Angela Hoy. Provides a free weekly newsletter full of useful information. I've gotten more than a few writing gigs from their listings. Also has a writing forum that's proven to be very supportive. Quarterly writing contest. Bookstore with lots of writing resources. And they provide ebook and POD publishing through their parent company, BookLocker.com. www.writersweekly.com/

Writing World – Moira Allen's website. Offers a free monthly newsletter as well as lots of writing information. www.writing-world.com/

WOW Women on Writing – Headed up by Angela MacIntosh. Provides a free monthly newsletter, writing contests, online classes and a Premium Green newsletter (available for $48 per year) that is so large I often don't make it all the way to the end. Premium Green offers a forum that is packed with information and support. wow-womenonwriting.com/

Individual state press associations

Most states have a newspaper association website. Often, you can find a directory of newspapers, along with other information such as names of editors and publishers, website and email addresses. Here are listings for individual state sites:

Newspaper Association of America – www.naa.org

Alabama Press Association
www.alabamapress.org

Alaska Newspaper Association
(no website)

Arizona Newspapers Association
www.ananews.com

Arkansas Press Association
www.arkansaspress.org

California Newspaper Publishers Association
www.cnpa.com

Colorado Press Association
www.coloradopressassociation.com

Connecticut – part of New England Newspaper & Press Association
www.nenpa.com

Florida Press Association
www.flpress.com

Georgia Press Association
www.gapress.org

Hoosier State Press Association
www.indianapublisher.com

Idaho Newspaper Association
www.idahopapers.com

Illinois Press Association
www.il-press.com

Iowa Press Association
www.inanews.com

Kansas Press Association
www.kspress.com

Kentucky Press Association
www.kypress.com

Louisiana Press Association
www.lapress.com

Maine Press Association
www.mainepress.wordpress.com

Maryland-Delaware-D.C. Press Association
www.mddcpress.com

Massachusetts Newspaper Publishers Association
www.masspublishers.org

Michigan Press Association
www.michiganpress.org

Minnesota Newspaper Association
www.mna.org

Mississippi Press Association
www.mspress.org

Missouri Press Association
www.mopress.com

Montana Newspaper Association
www.mtnewspapers.com

Nebraska Press Association
www.nebpress.com

Nevada Press Association
www.nevadapress.com

New England Newspaper & Press Association (Includes CT, ME, MS, NH, RI & VT)
www.nenpa.com

New Hampshire – part of New England Newspaper & Press Association
www.nenpa.com

New Jersey Press Association
www.njpa.org

New Mexico Press Association
www.nmpress.org

New York Newspaper Publishers Association
www.nynpa.com

New York Press Association
www.nynewspapers.com

North Carolina Press Association
www.ncpress.com

North Dakota Newspaper Association
www.ndna.com

Ohio Newspaper Association
www.ohionews.org

Oklahoma Press Association
www.okpress.com

Oregon Newspaper Publishers Association
www.orenews.com

Pennsylvania Newspaper Association
www.pa-newspaper.org

Rhode Island – part of New England Newspaper & Press Association
www.nenpa.com

South Carolina Press Association
www.scpress.org

South Dakota Newspaper Association
www.sdna.com

Tennessee Press Association
www.tnpress.com

Texas Daily Newspaper Association
www.tdna.org

Texas Press Association
www.texaspress.com

Utah Press Association
www.utahpress.com

Vermont – part of New England Newspaper & Press Association
www.nenpa.com

Virginia Press Association
www.vpa.net

Washington Newspaper Publishers Association
www.wnpa.com

West Virginia Press Association
www.wvpress.org

Wisconsin Newspaper Association
www.wnanews.com

Wyoming Press Association
www.wyopress.org

The Syndicates

If you want to pursue traditional syndication the old-fashioned way, you'll need contact information for the different syndication services. Here's a list of the five biggies (syndicates, that is):

• United Feature Syndicate – www.unitedfeatures.com/?title=Submissions

• King Features – www.kingfeatures.com/subg_column.htm

• Universal Press Syndicate – www.uexpress.com/submissions/

• Tribune Media Services – www.tribunemediaservices.com/ Submission guidelines: http://www.tmsfeatures.com/comicspage/

• Creators Syndicate – www.creators.com/submissions.html

And there's more

Here a site that lists 22 syndicates.
www.dmoz.org/news/media/services/syndicates/

Online sites that help you find syndicates

I don't vouch for these sites or promote them. I haven't ever used their services, so I don't know if they deliver or do what they say they can do. But they are a resource and they may work for you depending on your situation. So, check them out if you are interested. They are also good sources of free information regarding syndication and self-syndication. If nothing else, utilize them in that regard.

Market 2 Editors – Say they will help you syndicate your newspaper column. Lots of good (free) information. Fees based on weekly distribution. From my experience, it takes more than a few weeks for a newspaper to notice and publish a column. market2editors.com/

Publishers and Agents – Offshoot of Changemakers, Creative Communications & Research – Gini Scott, Ph.D., J.D. Help with querying and finding newspapers for syndication; looks like they focus on books and screenplays. Still they have some good (free) articles on syndication. www.publishersandagents.net/

Direct Contact PR – Run by Paul Krupkin. Offers various publicity services, including distribution of articles to a custom media list. www.directcontactpr.com/

Newspaper directories

There are directories (lots of them) that will sell you addresses for a fee. I recommend trying the state newspaper association websites first. Some of them have the actual emails on the state site, and all the information is free. If a particular state's association site isn't giving you the information you need, turn to one of these newspaper directories and work outward from there.

Newspaper directories will sell you addresses. But, you can use the free information on their site to access individual newspaper websites and find email addresses on your own. That's what I do. There are a number of directories out there. Here are a few to get you started.

With the sites listed below, you will have to access each individual newspaper website and then hunt and click to find email addresses.

Mondotimes.com – Information and links to newspapers. Organized by state.

Newslink.org – Links to online newspapers. Organized by state.

Directcontactpr.com/jumpstation/ – Media Jump Station: Links to online newspapers. Organized by state. Also offers news release services for a fee

USNPL.com – U.S. Newspaper List. Will give you click-on access to individual newspaper websites. Sells mailing addresses.

Newspaper Survey and Results

I conducted a highly unscientific survey of newspapers, asking various questions about columnists, budgets and the like. The results gave me some insight into the mind of the editor. I found them useful. I hope you do as well.

How often do columnists approach you?
1 – 6 times per year – 50%
Once or twice per month – 26%
Weekly – 14%

Preferred method of communication (email, phone snail mail etc.)?
Email – 100%

How often do you use freelance or syndicated columnists?
Weekly – 50%
Once or twice per month – 21%
Rarely – 29%

When approached, what makes you consider printing an article or column? Respondents were allowed to give multiple answers to this question. The percentages reflect number of respondents who gave each answer.
Subject matter of interest to readers – 57%
Cost – 43%
Quality of writing – 36%
One that I (editor or publisher) personally like – 36%
Reader feedback is positive – 29%
Need to fill space – 14%
Dependability – 14%
Length – 14%
Locally written – 14%

How much discretion do you have in your budget to pay columnists?
None – 45%
Some – 55%

Jill Pertler, a self-syndicated columnist, touches people's hearts and funny bones with the well-loved weekly column, *Slices of Life,* which appears in newspapers across the upper Midwest (and beyond). Jill lives in northern Minnesota, mainly because her family does and she'd miss them if she moved somewhere warmer, like Iowa. Still, a girl can dream. She shares her life, her home and just about everything else with her husband, four kids, a cat and dog. The dog snores. Her husband doesn't. Or is it the other way around? One thing's for sure: Jill doesn't snore and she loves hearing from happy readers. *Maybe that's two things…*

A portion of the proceeds from the sale of this book will be donated to the Cloquet Educational Foundation, an organization that provides learning opportunities for children from birth through high school – in the classroom and beyond.

LaVergne, TN USA
09 August 2010
192532LV00004B/24/P